paid!

paid!

**Reveals
The 10 Secrets for Being
Richly Rewarded
for the Value you Deliver**

PETER THOMSON

The
achievers
club

"Accelerates Your Business & Personal Growth"

*"This book is impossible to read—
I've tried several times and failed.*

Even getting to the end of a chapter is a struggle.

*It's packed with such a wealth of practical approaches,
brilliant ideas, and real-life solutions you have just have
to put it down and take immediate action.*

*Written in Peter's distinctive style, not business
book language, its instantly accessible and relatable
for any consultant or advisor wishing to move
their business forward.*

*So read it through once quickly, then read it a second
time slowly with a notebook book to hand for
your actions, but I doubt if you'll resist working on
them for long.*

*The advice and guidance here is of immeasurable value
and an incredible source of inspiration."*

Stephen Dann - Business Impact Solutions Ltd

Published by The Achievers Club Ltd

Book design & layout by Velin@Perseus-Design.com

978-1-7394271-0-8 – Paperback 6 x 9
978-1-7394271-3-9 – Hardback 6 x 9
978-1-7394271-1-5 – Hardback 8.25x11
978-1-7394271-2-2 – E-book

www.theachieversclub.com
www.thepaidbook.com

Contents

Foreword

Honoured!

That's what I felt when Peter asked me to write the foreword to this extraordinary book.

Let me explain...

I first encountered Peter in the 1990s when I was running my first business – an accounting firm. I remember subscribing to his audio newsletter, "The Achievers' Edge." It was pure gold (you will discover what that is as you read this book).

Peter became my inspiration, my mentor, and now a close friend.

I am incredibly privileged to have been able to build a 7-figure consulting business helping accountants and bookkeepers around the world. Peter played a key role in my professional development, career, and success.

I couldn't be where I am today without Peter.

And so, I feel profoundly blessed and honoured to have been asked to write the foreword to this book.

Anyway, enough about that; what about the book?

This book is full of practical insights you can implement straight away. It's full of insights that work.

For example, being an introverted accountant, I hated selling. I believed I couldn't sell. I remember the day clearly when I explained this to Peter, and he said something to me that was so profound. So profound it changed my outlook on selling completely... and now I love selling.

What was the advice?

You'll find out very soon. It's in the Introduction.

But don't just read the introduction. Read every chapter with care. Get ready to take notes. Get ready to take action on those notes. Get ready for the profound impact this book will have on your business.

Mark Wickersham, FCA

The most sought-after profit improvement expert in the accounting community, and author of many books, including "Value Pricing for Accounting Professionals".

Preface

Is **paid!** for you?

Yes, if you're someone who helps their clients solve problems or helps them capitalise on opportunities. Yes, if you get financially rewarded for the time you spend with them or the impact you create for them.

Over the last 30 years my clients have included consultants, coaches, owners of businesses of various sizes, accountants, speakers, trainers, authors, thoughts leaders and many others in a variety of professions.

They have been involved in widely differing sectors however each of them had similar thoughts about business and personal success.

- They were focused on creating positive outcomes for their clients

- They agreed it was right and fair to be amply rewarded for the value they create for their clients

paid!

- They accepted responsibility for their actions and enjoyed a positive mindset

If these ideas and ideals resonate with you, then **paid!** may just contain the ideas you've been seeking. Let's find out...

Throughout the book I've used 'consultant' as the person I'm talking about as I explain each idea. I know you'll be able to substitute your profession or activity to make each method and system applicable to you.

Professionals who would be helped by paid!

1. Business consultants
2. Professional garden designers
3. Accountants
4. Conference speakers
5. Financial advisors
6. Lawyers/Solicitors
7. Life coaches
8. Real estate agents
9. Psychologists/Psychotherapists
10. Career counsellors
11. Executive coaches
12. Management consultants
13. Marketing consultants
14. Public relations consultants
15. IT consultants
16. Personal trainers
17. Nutritionists/Dieticians
18. Social media consultants
19. HR consultants
20. Architects
21. Interior designers
22. Stylists (fashion, hair, makeup)
23. Private tutors
24. Wedding planners
25. Event planners
26. Medical consultants
27. Tax advisors
28. Private investigators
29. Personal shoppers
30. Art consultants
31. Corporate trainers
32. Speech therapists
33. Music therapists
34. Health and safety consultants
35. Audiologists
36. Data analysts
37. Family therapists
38. Mediators
39. Environmental consultants
40. SEO consultants
41. Research consultants
42. Branding consultants
43. Image consultants
44. Feng Shui consultants

45. Immigration consultants
46. Communications consultants
47. Investment consultants
48. Software consultants
49. Customer service consultants
50. Education consultants
51. Motivational speakers
52. Patent agents
53. Political consultants
54. Travel consultants
55. Guitar teachers
56. Piano tutors
57. Dance instructors
58. Vocal coaches
59. Drama teachers
60. Yoga instructors
61. Pilates instructors
62. Art teachers
63. Photographers
64. Hypnotherapists
65. Physiotherapists
66. Chiropractors
67. Occupational therapists
68. Opticians
69. Podiatrists
70. Dermatologists
71. Aesthetic practitioners
72. Veterinarians
73. Sommeliers
74. Language tutors
75. Chess coaches
76. Astrologers
77. Feng Shui experts
78. Personal chefs
79. Wine consultants
80. Sleep consultants
81. Parenting coaches
82. Lactation consultants
83. Home organisation experts
84. Elder care consultants
85. Relationship coaches
86. Bereavement counsellors
87. Translators
88. Proofreaders
89. Dog trainers
90. Horse riding instructors
91. Scuba diving instructors
92. Driving instructors
93. Ski instructors
94. Masseuses/Masseurs
95. Acupuncturists
96. Reiki practitioners
97. Holistic health consultants
98. Sound therapists
99. Midwives/Doulas
100. Genealogists

Templates

To make this as easy as possible for you to take action with the ideas and methods you'll discover throughout paid!, I've created a number of templates.

These are the templates I use in my private practice and those I share with my clients.

Go to: www.thepaidbook.com/downloads where you can access them.

If you have any questions about the use of the templates email success@peterthomson.com

Disclaimer

This book, **paid!** ("the Book"), is intended to provide general information and guidance for readers seeking to be rightfully rewarded for the value they bring to their clients. The author and publisher have made every effort to ensure that the information contained herein is accurate and up-to-date as of the publication date. However, the Book is not intended to serve as a substitute for professional advice, and neither the author nor the publisher assumes any responsibility for any actions taken or not taken by readers based on the content of this Book.

The strategies, tips, and insights presented in the Book are not guaranteed to produce specific results or outcomes for every individual reader. The success of each reader will depend on various factors, including personal and professional circumstances, market conditions, and the specific business environment in which they operate.

While the author has drawn from personal experience and that of others in writing this Book, it is essential for readers to understand that every situation is unique. Readers should consider their specific circumstances and

paid!

consult with appropriate professionals, such as legal or financial advisors, before implementing any strategies or recommendations contained in the Book.

By reading this Book, you agree to assume full responsibility for your actions and decisions and absolve the author and publisher from any liability arising from the use or misuse of the information provided. The author and publisher make no representations or warranties, express or implied, with respect to the accuracy, reliability, or completeness of the information contained in this Book, and specifically disclaim any implied warranties of merchantability or fitness for a particular purpose.

The author and publisher reserve the right to modify, alter, or update the content of this Book without notice, and they are not responsible for any errors, omissions, or inaccuracies that may occur after the publication date. Any such changes will be reflected in subsequent editions of the Book.

"Money is the silent reward
For a job well done and
Value delivered to others"

Introduction

Of all the challenges facing highly-skilled professionals, the one standing head and shoulders above the rest is:

How to get rightfully, richly and regularly rewarded for the value they deliver

Sadly, most professional consultants are still undercharging; charging fees that are far too low considering the positive impact they make on their clients' lives.

Let's dive into this problem now and solve it together...

Come with me now as we examine...

- The 2 Attribution Errors - and how, by avoiding them, we set ourselves up for greater deserved success

- The Belief/Action conundrum and how to get this working in your favour

paid!

- The 6 Proven Pricing Models and how to maximise value for your clients and maximise income for yourself

- The 4 Golden Questions of Business Growth
  And 12 answers you can implement immediately

- Why writing your Business Book – is a must

- Magnetic Lead Generation.
  How to attract <u>only</u> those clients you love to work with

- How to position yourself and your fees to increase client engagements

- How to build a business and a 'Life of Choice' – your choice

- Ongoing help and guidance

It's going to be fun – with very serious intent.

The Essential Mindset

Change Your Life

This is very easy to say. It is very easy to understand. Yet, it seems to take some people ages to fully integrate this critically important idea into their whole being, into their identity, and into their actions.

I urge you to take this on board...

Once this fully resonates with who you are (your identity), every time you interact with a prospect or client, you'll do so from a position of strength. One where you feel relaxed, confident and in control.

Even if you stopped reading after knowing this - you would be better prepared to engage more clients who are ready, willing and able to pay you for the value you deliver to them.

I cannot stress enough how important this idea is to your success.

> *"Learn how to sell, then stop selling*
> *and allow people to buy"*
>
> Peter Thomson

You do not need to spend any time whatsoever trying to 'convince' people to do something they do <u>not</u> want to do.

Just don't do it!

Instead, increase your ability to be 'convincing'.

It's easier, smoother, honest and integrity-laden: the way to live your life of choice. Oh yes!

More later...

Let's get going...

CHAPTER ONE

The Attribution Errors

The Fundamental Attribution Error

We judge <u>others</u> by their <u>actions</u>;
we judge <u>ourselves</u> by our <u>intentions</u>

Far too often, we can be guilty of layering someone's actions onto their identity.

For example:

1. A person turns up late for a meeting. We whisper to a colleague, "They <u>are</u> always late."

2. <u>We</u> turn up late for a meeting and exclaim, "The traffic out there is crazy."

In example #1, we have stated who the person is by using the verb 'to be' (they are). That's their identity. They are a 'late person'.

In example #2 - we have excused ourselves by placing the blame on an outside agency - the traffic. And by doing so, we have avoided taking responsibility for our actions. And we have maintained our identity as someone who usually turns up on time.

There's a difference between being drunk and being a drunk!

Let's exercise some care in attributing the action to the identity. It can stick and do untold damage long term.

This labelling effect is also very potent when we consider attracting those clients we love to help.

When we clearly describe who we want to help in language that resonates with their identity and past actions - we attract those people to our message.

It's been said there are two ways to attract those clients we love to work with.

#1: Spend time and money advertising (and this certainly works)

#2: Become so attractive, so enthused about what you do, that clients will find you.

I prefer to use both strategies.

The Pricing Attribution Error

This mistake has so many downsides:

1. Reduction of potential income
2. Lack of 'belief in us' by clients
3. Unnecessary extra time spent in the business
4. Poor positioning in our chosen marketplace
5. Lower significance in our own eyes

Here's how the problem occurs...

A consultant (Let's call him John) decides how to set his fee rate (often a daily rate) by valuing himself and his time. Sometimes John may add a small amount extra to allow for a bit more profit.

Don't do that!

Set your fees, <u>not</u> by the value of your day, but <u>by the value of the benefits your client receives</u> from your intervention, your advice, and your help.

The challenge you and I face (as well as every other professional) is coming to terms with the value of our time.

"You will never get paid more than you truly believe you are worth"

Peter Thomson

Our beliefs change...

Fortunately, as time goes by and we test different (and higher) fees, our belief in our value increases as new clients readily accept them.

> *"Until you value yourself, you won't value your time. Until you value your time, you will not do anything with it"*
>
> M Scott Peck

I recall being at a seminar many years ago where I was the MC and a speaker. After my session, a businessman approached me and asked if I would be willing to help him grow his business. He was very interested in me training his sales team members to be more successful.

He asked how much my day rate was. And, because I'd been considering raising my fees, and this was the first opportunity to test my new price, I quoted 2.5 times my normal rate.

He readily accepted!

Of course, that made me think I should have quoted even higher!

I went on to do over £300,000 of business with that company. That was £180,000 more than I would have received at my old rate.

The Attribution Errors

As the company's turnover increased by over £10,000,000 due to implementing the ideas we discussed (and other actions), I rightfully felt everyone had received good value for money.

Jeff Pettitt, a professional referee and businessman, stated:

> *"Most people reach the limit of their belief well before they reach the limit of their talent"*

Let's imagine you work only on a contingency basis. (I'm not saying you should, and we'll come back to this later)

You receive a commission on your client's increased financial results by t hem using your ideas.

Example A:
The client gains an extra £10,000 in profit.
Would it be fair and reasonable for you to be paid a £1,000 (10%) commission? Yes, of course, it would.

Example B:
The client gains an extra £100,000 in profit.
Would it be fair and reasonable for you to be paid a £10,000 (10%) commission? Yes, of course, it would.

Example C:
The client gains an extra £1,000,000 in profit
Would it be fair and reasonable for you to be paid a £100,000 (10%) commission? Yes, of course, it would.

paid!

So, why would we charge the same 'fee rate' when the values received by our clients can vary so considerably?

And, even if we spent the same amount of time with the client to explain our ideas.

"You Don't Get Paid for the Hour.
You Get Paid for the Value
You Bring to the Hour"
Jim Rohn

This is Price Pliability

Simply with this in mind, we begin to realise the value of our ideas.

You may prefer to work on a fee rate basis. Or charge on a project basis. However, starting by considering the value you deliver rather than the time you spend will create the mindset of your value to the client.

"It's Not the Hours You Put in,
it's What You Put in Those Hours"
Peter Thomson

Now let's go up to the next level:

The Value of the Value.

This sounds a little unusual, so let me explain.

If the value you deliver in monetary terms is, say, £100,000, then the next level question is, "What's the value of that value?"

Clarity:

Your client gains an extra £100,000 using your ideas. That money is just bits of paper or numbers on a computer.

What's the <u>real value</u> of this £100,000 to your client?

Is it a greater feeling of security? Is it a new car, home, holiday, presents for partner and children, time to enjoy other activities, or care for an elderly relative? Or...

What's the Value of the Value you deliver?

It will be worth writing this down.

Now we are getting to realise the true difference our ideas make to our clients' lives and why they will gladly pay our fair and reasonable <u>pliable</u> fee rates.

Increasing your earnings is like climbing a mountain. The journey might be challenging, but the view from the top is worth every step.

Note: all of these ideas are based on 'value delivered'. We never try to use any underhand or sleazy tactics to rip off unsuspecting people. That's not who we are or what we do.

When we focus on value, our clients and prospects feel this focus in everything we say and do. In every word, we say or write. In every expression or gesture.

Far better to build a business in this way. One we can be proud of. One where we can look back and say, "Yes, I did it. I made a positive difference in the world."

> *"My motto has always been,*
> *only first-class business*
> *and that in a first-class way"*
> David Ogilvy

A wonderful thought to take on board, isn't it?

The Advice-Giving Effect:

There is real power in this idea. In essence, when we show someone else how to do something, we are also showing ourselves. And reminding ourselves to do what we advise.

Based on this simple explanation: what would you advise someone like you to charge as their fee rate? (Answer in the table below)

The Attribution Errors

Questions	Answers
What's the value of the value?	
What is a day of your life worth?	
How much are your ideas worth?	
What would you advise someone else to charge?	
How much will your new fee rate be?	
How often will you test it?	
And how often will you increase it?	
How soon will you implement your new fee rate?	

Did I hear you say, "Now!"

"That's great news, do let me know how you get on!"
success@peterthomson.com

REFRESHER 1

1. The Fundamental Attribution Error. We judge others by their actions we judge ourselves by our intentions.

2. The Pricing Attribution Error. Setting at fees by the time we spend rather than the impact we have and the value we deliver.

3. Price Pliability. It's not the hours you put in it what you put in the hours.

4. The Value of the Value. What will your clients do with the extra income your ideas and guidance has brought them?

5. The Advice Giving Affect. Consider how you would answer someone else's questions if they had the same challenges/opportunities you have.

In the next chapter, we'll look at: Positioning, Power and Persuasion.

And examine a variety of ways of creating a presence and brand in our chosen marketplace.

And, if you've ever struggled to boldly state why a client should pick you as their 'go to person' then the Carton Concept will be a revelation.

CHAPTER TWO

Positioning Power Persuasion

Three of the important factors in how we get rightfully rewarded for the difference we make are:

1. How we are positioned both in the marketplace and in our potential clients' minds

2. Our personal power and how we use it and

3. How we use ethical persuasion methods to serve our clients' best interests and still be regarded as the 'go to person' in our industry

In this chapter, I'm going to share with you a variety of tried and tested and proven ideas in these 3 critical areas.

1. Positioning:

Author Status:

A strange thing happens as soon as we become an author. It is that our feeling of self-worth increases. And this new level of confidence shines out of our eyes and through everything we say and do.

In my business, part of my offering is to help people write and create informational products, usually starting with a book.

I'm always so pleased to see how differently a new author walks into a room. Their heads are held high, their shoulders are back, they are smiling confidently, and everything about them has changed (for the better).

Is this any wonder when we realise the word 'authority' contains the word 'author'. Yes, we are perceived as an <u>authority</u> as soon as we have written and either published or printed our book. (I urge you to become an author).

Later, I will explain even more about writing and creating your own book. And a variety of ways you can use the information you've captured in the book to develop even more informational products to help you get your clients to get the outcomes they want.

The Tray Exercise:

Let's have some fun!

Follow along with me as I explain to you a fun exercise I've carried out with audiences across the world, so they can realise the power of a major factor in positioning, power and persuasion.

Imagine, for a moment, I'm holding a tea tray. (When I'm doing this from a stage, I don't have a tea tray; I'm just holding my hands out as though I were holding one)

Here is my description of the tray.

It's made of wood. It's black and highly polished. On it is a dragon design, highly colourful and decorative.

It's for sale in a mid-range department store.

I'd like you to think about and decide on what would be the price of the ticket for that tray in that location. Write your number in this box.

```
┌─────────────────────────────────────┐
│                                       │
│                                       │
│                                       │
└─────────────────────────────────────┘
```

Now, let's imagine that this tray is for sale in a car boot or garage sale. It's still the same tray. It's still brand new. It's still in its original wrapping.

paid!

What is the price of this tray in the car boot or garage sale? Write your number in this box.

```
┌─────────────────────────────────────────┐
│                                         │
│                                         │
│                                         │
└─────────────────────────────────────────┘
```

And for the third time. Let's imagine the tray is now for sale in the most expensive store you know. This might be Harrods in London, perhaps Macy's in the USA. The tray is still brand-new. It's still in its original wrapping.

What is the price of the tray now that it's for sale in Harrods or Macy's? Write your number in this box.

```
┌─────────────────────────────────────────┐
│                                         │
│                                         │
│                                         │
└─────────────────────────────────────────┘
```

Now, if you are at all like the thousands of people I've shared this idea with, then you had probably put a mid-range price for the tray when it was for sale in the mid-range Department store.

You've probably put a much lower price when it was for sale in the car boot sale or garage sale.

And you probably put a much higher price when it was for sale in Harrods in the UK or Macy's in the USA. Is that right?

Yes, then it begs this question, "Why?". Why did the price change in most people's minds from mid-range to low to high?

Positioning Power Persuasion

Write your ideas in this box:

Over the years I've shared this idea, I've heard many different ideas. Perception, experience, location, and many others.

However, the major factor that changes the 'price perception' in the eyes and mind of the potential buyer –is the 'brand' of the supplier.

The Supplier Brand

If this is true, and I believe it to be so, then we must definitely consider the factors that create this 'Supplier Brand' and then consider how we will score in each of those factors.

Here are some thoughts for you to consider.

I'd also like you to write down any other ideas you have regarding the factors in the Supplier Brand.

Trust, reputation, location, testimonials, previous experiences, social media reports, time in business and website. And I'm sure you can think of many more.

paid!

Here is my suggestion. Write down a list of the factors you feel are relevant for you in your industry and marketplace, and then allocate a score for each factor out of a maximum of 10 points.

You will easily see where you feel there are changes or improvements to be made.

Factors	Score
1	
2	
3	
4	
5	
6	
7	
8	
9	
10	
Notes	

Relational versus Transactional:

Some years ago, I was fortunate to interview Roy H Williams, known as The Wizard of Ads. I feel I learnt more in the 40 minutes we were together than in any other 40 minutes in my life.

He shared one particular idea with me, which I have since shared with many of my clients, and it has made such a difference to both my life and theirs.

I'd like to share it with you now.

Roy stated there is a great deal of difference between the Relational Client and the Transactional Customer.

He explained that the transactional customer is their own expert and tends to buy on price. It is purely a transaction.

For example, let's say a person has decided to buy a new car. They know all the specs and all the details. They know everything they need to know about the car.

They contact three different dealers and play one off against the others in order to get the lowest possible price. As Roy explained, the only way you could upset this person is to tell them they could've purchased the car £10 cheaper somewhere else once they've bought the car.

I don't know about you, but I have no interest in attracting transactional customers. They do not fit my typical avatar or relate to my ideas about value rather than price. Is that the same for you?

Now here's the real insight I learned from Roy.

The relational client expects the supplier to be the expert. And whilst price is a factor, it's <u>not</u> the factor.

This is perfect for professionals. You and I share our knowledge, experience, expertise and our 'take' on those, and we have already discussed how we sell on the value of the value rather than the price of time. Ideally, this is suited for the 'relational client' who looks to us as the expert and delivers the value they want.

How would we describe this relational client?

Well, in the words of Michael Basch, they stay, they pay, and they say. They are happy paying 'the right price', and they pay on time. They stay for a long time. And they happily tell others about their experiences as one of our clients. In other words, they are referral conscious.

These are surely the ideal clients you and I want.

I would urge you to think carefully about who you want to attract and set your stall out accordingly.

Another 3 factors in determining price:

We want to continue to test to find the level of pricing that attracts exactly the people we want to deal with and at a price that they are happy, willing and able to pay.

Let's consider two different careers.

On the one hand, we have a road sweeper. On the other hand, we have a surgeon.

Now, I am not comparing the people. People have a choice as to what they decide to do with their lives, and while some would claim that the circumstances will be different for the 'sweeper' than for the 'surgeon,' it is purely the financial implication we are considering.

Here are the 3 factors:

1. How hard the job is to learn
2. How long it takes to learn
3. How difficult the person is to replace in the function

As we can see. It doesn't take long to learn how to be a road sweeper. Whilst it is a physically demanding job, it isn't hard to learn. And I think we would probably agree that finding a replacement would be easier than finding many other positions.

And the difference for the surgeon?

It takes a long time to learn to be a surgeon. It is a difficult learning experience, highly detailed. And certainly not an easy position to refill.

Whilst the surgeon won't be the only surgeon in the world, the more specialised they become, the more they create a position or category of 'one'.

And this is precisely what we need to do too. We need to be so specific about who we help, how we help them and how we are different that we establish our very own 'Category of One'.

Therefore, we are not surprised the surgeon is far more highly paid than the road sweeper.

When you and I look at what we do, helping our clients to either solve the problems they encounter or capitalise on the opportunities that present themselves - we realise on a scale from 'road sweepers to surgeons', we must certainly be sited at the higher levels.

It takes a long time to learn to do what we do. That learning curve is steep (hard). And we are not easily replaced.

No wonder we charge some of the highest hourly/daily rates. And rightfully so. After all, as I mentioned earlier:

"Money is the Silent Applause for a Job Well Done and Value Delivered to Others"

Peter Thomson

The Importance of Straplines:

To make certain, we separate ourselves and our products from the enormous amount of other offerings in the marketplace, it is essential we have a strapline for ourselves and for our products.

Positioning Power Persuasion

The strapline can be in three different styles and sometimes even an amalgamation of two or all of these ideas.

1. A statement of who we are
2. A statement of what we do
3. A description of the benefit the client experiences by using our services or products

Examples:

One of the straplines I regularly use is:
"The U.K.'s Most Prolific Information Product Creator"

This is simply a statement of who I am!

Sometimes, particularly on banners I use at seminars, it states:

Peter Thomson
"Turns your knowledge experience and expertise into ongoing streams of cash."

This combination clearly states what I <u>do</u> and the <u>benefit</u> my clients receive.

Product strapline examples:

Some years ago, I created a product called: The Accelerated Business Growth System. And wrote a strapline as follows: "Turns your business into a well-oiled profit generating machine." This might be a little 'cute'; it certainly worked as we were able to sell many copies of the programme at a substantial profit.

paid!

One of the mentoring groups I run is called: The Adventures. Its strapline is: "The Courage to Succeed". As you can see, this focuses on the labelling of the Members as being courageous individuals.

My suggestion is: you create a strapline for yourself that clearly positions you. And you create a strapline for every service or product you supply using the ideas I've covered.

I particularly like straplines for products and services which clearly detail the benefits the client will receive.

Your website:

One of the great lessons I've learnt about websites is that every page must have its own reason for being there, and the majority of pages have their own MWA. This stands for Most Wanted Action.

For example, on the homepage of my website, I know my most wanted action is for me to give every visitor a valuable information product to start our relationship and for them to reciprocate by giving me their contact details.

Almost always, I use one of my books (either as a physical product sent in the post or a PDF version) as the 'ethical bribe' for the visitor to give me their details.

If we always consider our website part of our marketing process and not simply a brochure, then we are far more likely to create one that gives value to the visitor and performs the most wanted action.

2. Power:

Now let's look at the various factors in establishing our power in the marketplace.

CBA:

Confidence: when we have complete confidence in ourselves and our ability to deliver our ideas, methods and proven processes to our clients, this will transmit itself in all our communications.

Belief: when we have complete belief in the efficacy of our ideas, this too will shine through all of our interactions.

Alignment: as we now know, people will never consistently do who they aren't; then we realise the only way to be successful as a professional (or in any other field of endeavour) is to make certain our actions are in alignment with those beliefs, values and our identity.

My suggestion is you consider a score out of 10 for yourself in each of these 3 critical areas: confidence, belief and alignment.

If you find you are not able to score at a high level, then you consider what you can do to increase your score or question yourself as to whether or not you are in the right place, doing what you love.

Professor Robert Cialdini, the author of the best-selling book, Influence The Psychology of Persuasion, is renowned as the world's leading authority in the art and science of persuasion.

I had an opportunity to interview him when he visited London, and in the interview, he explained to me the major ideas of his work.

His concept of authority is one of those ideas relevant to establishing our power.

He stated for someone to be perceived as an authority, there are three factors.

1. Title
2. Trappings
3. Clothing

This links perfectly with the other ideas we've been discussing.

It's necessary for us to have a title. We've covered this in the idea of creating a strapline for ourselves that we can use on the products or services, on our website and business card and in any introduction.

Trappings will be such things as our briefcase, pen, paperwork, brochures, and even the car we drive.

All of these items will have an impact on how someone else perceives us as an authority figure.

An old expression says, "To be well dressed is to be appropriately dressed". And this is so true when we talk about authority.

Positioning Power Persuasion

You and I have seen people in uniform who are immediately treated as an authority figure. For example, a police officer, a pilot, a doctor, a nurse, and even someone wearing a high-vis jacket.

Imagine for a moment...

You are driving down a dark country lane one evening in November. It's raining, and visibility is low. Then, there in front of you, you notice somebody in the road. And as you get closer, you realise it's a young man standing by his car with his hand raised in a typical stop signal.

What's your feeling about this? Are you going to stop? Are you concerned or nervous? Suspicious? I'm certain you would be careful in those circumstances.

Just imagine another night, still in November, still poor visibility. Then there, in the distance, we see a car. It's a police car with its light flashing. There is a man in a police uniform standing in the middle of the road with his right hand raised, palm towards us, in a typical "Stop!" gesture.

What would we do? Almost certainly, we would stop.

What a difference a flashing light and a uniform make.

This is the power of title, trappings and clothing, and we must ensure that we use them to the best effect to demonstrate our authority and power in the marketplace.

3. Persuasion:

Here are a variety of ways in which you can be more persuasive when dealing with your prospects and clients. This, of course, it's still on the basis that we learn how to sell, stop selling and allow people to buy.

Over the last 30 years, as I've been helping coaches, consultants, speakers, trainers and small business owners to become more successful, particularly in the area of pricing and charges -I've found the biggest challenge they face is talking about their price or fee when the client asks the "How much?" question.

They stutter, they stumble, they feel embarrassed, and their concern about the fee rate leaks out of every action, every word, every gesture.

Here's how to solve this problem once and for all...

It's a metaphor.

Get a large box. Give the box a transformational name relevant to the benefits a client gets from your intervention/help. Give the box a strapline which adds to the persuasiveness of the name. Put yourself in the box. And then...

Sell the box!

Now, you can talk about the box and its contents. How brilliant the contents are and how they will help your client get the desired outcome. You can describe the features, the factors, the benefits and why the box has been 'constructed' in this way.

Years ago, when I first started the consulting and mentoring business, I interviewed the owner of an American company called Future World, Dr Dan Lee Dimke.

As I was having some small struggles in describing both myself and the benefits I could bring to the client, I asked Dan's advice. He gave me a brilliant suggestion. He said, "Imagine you're talking about somebody else. Describe them and how helpful they can be and all the successes they've had in the past."

Following this advice, I bought for the members of one of my mentoring groups, small wooden figures. You know, the type where the arms, legs and head are movable. The type often used by artists and sculptors.

I asked the mentoring group members to imagine they were the wooden figures and describe the successes, the services, the benefits, the pricing, the fees - everything about them.

They found it so easy. This 'disassociating technique' works brilliantly!

So, if you've ever had any difficulty describing what you do, the benefits the client gets, and the fee you want, then simply "Put yourself in the box!"

Reciprocation:

Another of the factors of persuasion described by Professor Robert Cialdini is the idea of reciprocation and obligation. You and I know it's far better to give before we ask. And one of the better ways we can do this, in a client conversation, is to give the client a copy of your book.

Later in this book, I'll be explaining more about how simple (though not necessarily easy) it is to write your own business book; and how essential this is to your success.

If you've not yet written your book, you could start a meeting with a client by giving them a book you highly recommend.

After the pleasantries have taken place, coffee has been offered and you've discussed the state of the nation, it's time to get down to business and to start the meeting in such a friendly and reciprocation-inducing way, we simply say: "This is my latest book, I thought you might like a copy."

I have never, ever had a prospect or client do other than thank me and take the book. I wait.

They will take a moment to look at the front cover and the back cover (where there is information about me, my previous successes, my history in business and the content and benefits of the book.) They may even open the book and start reading some of the pages.

This is when in a very calm, quiet voice, I ask, "Would you like me to sign it for you?" Now, I realise this is a very bold move and one that will only work if we are completely confident in delivering this line.

Over many years of doing this, I've never had anybody say, "No". In fact, everyone has smiled and said, "Yes, please". What has this done to my positioning in the client's eyes? Everything I could possibly wish.

I've also never experienced a client meeting where I have offered the book and asked if they like me to sign it where I did not do some form of business with them either then or shortly thereafter.

Now you know why I believe it is absolutely essential you and every coach, consultant, speaker, trainer, accountant, business owner, entrepreneur, and I, must, I repeat, must be the author of a business book. (More about this later)

Social Proof:

I'm certain you've used testimonials, case studies and reference sites (clients who can be called for reference and testimonials) in your business. And all of those fall under the title of 'Social proof'.

The growth of review sites and social media has seen the idea of social proof rise to entirely new levels, where most people will check to see what other purchasers say about a product or service before making the decision to buy.

We can use the power of social proof in our client engagement conversations.

How do we get testimonials? We ask for them.

Powerful testimonials can be crafted along the following lines. Yes, it's better to have testimonials in the client's own words; however, sometimes, clients need help and advice to be able to write their thoughts.

1. What was the problem happening in the client's life before the product or service was supplied
2. What was the downside they were experiencing because of the problem
3. Details about the product/service they bought
4. Details about the benefits or experiences they enjoyed
5. The recommendation that someone should also buy the product/service

Commitment Consistency

Another factor of influence Professor Robert Cialdini mentioned in both the interview I carried out with him and his books is the idea of 'commitment consistency'.

I feel this is the most misunderstood of the ideas he talks about. And this is not because of the way he talks about them, no! Simply because of the idea itself of 'commitment consistency'.

What does 'commitment consistency' mean?

It simply means that people tend to remain consistent with previously made commitments. And in particular, when those commitments are non-forced and publicly made.

Let me give you an example.

We ask potential clients about previous training they've undertaken or previous help they've received from a consultant. We find out which part of that training of consultancy worked for them - and the benefits they received.

We are confirming their previous commitments to training and consultancy help.

We can also discover what parts of the training/consultancy they enjoyed, how it worked, and how many facets will help us remind them of their previous enjoyment and previous commitment.

How do we use commitment and consistency?

You are well aware of my thoughts about selling. Inasmuch as I believe we need to learn how to sell, stop selling, and then allow people to buy.

However, let me add to this:

"Selling takes place in the gathering stage as people sell themselves in their answers to your well-crafted questions"

Peter Thomson

If this is true, and I fervently believe it is, then it is essential we create our questions with careful thought as to the likely <u>mood</u> the prospect will be placed into by their answers. And the likely thinking <u>mode</u> they will enter because of their answers.

My experience tells me very few consultants, and fellow professionals take the time to carefully craft the questions they are about to ask the client when engaging in the first meeting.

You and I are different!

Let's link this back to 'commitment consistency'.

A number of other questions need to be asked of a potential client to uncover their previously made commitments. So that we are able to (ethically) align our offering and offer to those previously made commitments.

Why? Because they are far more likely to agree to go ahead.

You note I said ethically!

The questions we can ask our clients will be along the lines of the following:

"Can you tell me about other training you've undertaken?". "Can you explain to me how a coach or consultant has helped you in the past?"

You can see how these questions will confirm that the potential client has previously taken training in the past and has been helped by a coach or consultant.

What we're looking to do, is just to remind the client of their previously made commitments (non-forced) so when we come to explain how we can help them, we are not asking them to become a different person (identity); we are asking them to maintain 'who they are' and, stay in alignment with 'what they have previously done'.

Clues in the Office:

Most professional salespeople (and that's you and me) are well versed in entering a new client's office and carefully looking around to find out more information about the client and their interests to build rapport with our comments and questions. Agreed?

This is exactly the same.

Scarcity:

Another powerful factor in the selling and buying process is the idea of – scarcity.

Let's look at how this works.

Imagine you're driving home one day and listening to the radio when you hear the news announcement that there's going to be a major shortage of sugar. What is likely to happen when the population hears this announcement?

You and I know the answer. Yes, there will be a rush to the shops to buy and hoard sugar. The very announcement about scarcity created scarcity.

Scarcity is a powerful tool. Of the nine major factors that Professor Robert Cialdini talks about, the one that truly creates immediate action is – scarcity.

So, what ethical, integrity-based scarcity can we use?

First, you and I are a scarce resource. We only have a certain number of days we are prepared to allocate to work with clients. Therefore, the true scarcity is time. And showing your client a full diary will immediately create a feeling of scarcity.

If we were offering a subscription programme, we might decide we would only allow a certain number of people to join or allow everyone to join within a certain period of time. Those are two different types of scarcity.

If we were offering our informational products online, we might decide to add a bonus that is only available for a certain number of people or a certain amount of time.

All of these are fair and reasonable scarcities.

The Scarcity Mistake:

You have seen, as I have, people offering 'scarce items' in their marketing, and we know full well that these items are not scarce. In the same way, the value of bonuses is inflated in so many marketing messages, and all this does is destroy the credibility of the person making the offer.

So, any scarcity we decide to use must be honest and believable, and any scarcity stated must be held to. For example, if we say a certain bonus is only available for a certain period of time, then we must remove the bonus at the end of the time period.

If we say that only a certain number of people can join during our membership launch programme, then we must stick to this figure and not use any 'weasel words' to get around this previously made commitment.

Scarcity is a very powerful tool and, when used properly and with integrity, can produce excellent results in our persuasive conversations with our prospects and clients.

Like any powerful tool - it must be used with care.

In my Private Practice:

This four-word expression is extremely compelling and great positioning for who we are and what we do. Because of that, it adds to the persuasion process.

Example:

"In my private practice, I only deal with five major clients at any one time. This is because of the amount of mental focus I give to each of those clients and the amount of time I want to spend with them to get them the outcomes they came to me for, in the first place."

What wonderful positioning - and with a hefty dose of 'scarcity'!

My suggestion is you take time to go through all of the ideas in this chapter again and again until they match with who you are (identity) and that with sufficient practice, you're able to deliver all the words you use as fluently, eloquently and persuasively as possible.

You and I want to attract the 'relational client' who looks to us to be the expert. Fortunately, when we do this, price becomes only a factor and not the factor in any client conversation.

REFRESHER 2

1. Positioning Power Persuasion

2. Benefitting from author status.

3. The Tray Exercise. The importance of your brand in how people view you and your fees.

4. Relational versus Transactional. Attracting the relational client rather than the transactional customer.

5. Another 3 factors in determining price. How hard to learn, how long to learn, difficulty to replace.

6. Money is the silent applause for a job well done and value delivered to others.

7. The Importance of Strap Lines. Create strap lines for yourself and for your products and services.

8. Most Wanted Action. Making certain this is clear on your website.

9. Confidence, Belief and Alignment.

10. Authority Figures. Title, trappings and clothing.

11. Sell the Box! Make it easy to describe who you are and what are you do by describing yourself as a product rather than a service.

12. Reciprocation. Give a new client a copy of your latest book/report.

13. Social Proof. Get testimonials from your satisfied clients.

14. Commitment Consistency. Ask questions to discover what potential clients have committed to in the past so you can ethically align your offering.

15. Selling takes place in the gathering stage as people sell themselves in their answers to your well crafted questions.

16. Scarcity. What true scarcity can you add to your offering?

17. In My Private Practice. Excellent positioning for you and your offering.

In the next chapter, we will explore the concept of "skin in the game" and address the limitations of most training programs while providing effective solutions to overcome these challenges.

Action Plan

Actions	Priority	When by	Done

CHAPTER THREE

Skin in The Game

Over 30 years ago, I pondered:

> *"Why do some people fail*
> *to succeed to the level of success,*
> *that their level of skill*
> *indicates they could achieve?"*

And I realised, in the majority of cases, there was a mismatch between <u>what</u> and <u>who.</u>

What they were asked, or asked themselves, to do (behaviour) - and who they believed themselves to be (identity).

Those two major elements were out of sync.

And so, I created this expression:

> ## "People will never consistently <u>do</u> who they <u>aren't</u>!"
>
> Peter Thomson

You will have seen people attend a training course and return to the workplace full of enthusiasm. They seem to be happy using their new skills. Their attitude is more positive than before.

Then, within a short space of time - they return to the behaviours and attitudes of the past.

Why?

The mismatch between <u>who</u> they are and <u>what</u> they're being asked to do.

This is one of the major reasons why training doesn't have a long-term impact.

Training can work on a long-term basis if sufficient time is spent aligning the new skills with the <u>identity</u> of the person being trained.

This mismatch problem also creates difficulties when we are setting our fee rates.

Important Note:

If you feel you aren't worth a certain fee rate or do not deserve a level of income – then you will never consistently take the necessary actions to increase your earnings.

Every time you consider asking for a higher fee rate (a justified increase), your inner voice will express your doubts, and just as you're about to ask, you'll revert to your 'standard rate'.

This will only change when you have decided you are worth the rate you charge.

DECIDE!

Note: the word 'decide' originates from the Middle English deciden, from the Middle French decider from the Latin decidere literally, to cut off. In other words, when you 'decide', you have cut yourself off from any other idea. You have decided.

DECIDE!

This poem by Jesse B Rittenhouse reminds us that there is no shortage of money, no! There is a shortage of people who <u>decide</u> how much they want and then (bear the task) continue to take action until they achieve their goal (and beyond).

paid!

My Wage

I bargained with Life for a penny
And life would pay no more
However, I begged in the evening
When I counted my scanty store

For Life is a just employer
He gives you what you ask
But, once you have set the wages
Why, you must bear the task

I worked for a menial's hire
Only to learn, dismayed
That any wage I had asked of Life
Life would have willingly paid.

One of the BIGGEST mistakes:

Some people consider the way to be successful (by whatever their definition of that emotive word - success) is...

1. To <u>have</u> 'stuff'
2. So they can <u>do</u> things
3. So they can be a certain person

WRONG!

Completely the wrong way around.

Here's the way it really works:

Skin in The Game

1. We must be the person we wish to become

2. We do the actions that type of person does
   - We act the way that type of person acts
   - We walk the way that person walks
   - We talk the way that person talks
   - We set our goals
   - We work towards those goals on a daily basis
   - We maintain our positive attitude in the face of difficulty

And none of these cost any money or extra time.

3. Then – we will have the outcomes that type of person has:
   1. The income level we have decided upon
   2. The position in our organisation or business we always wanted
   3. The level of recognition, respect and significance we desire
   4. Anything and everything we set our heart and mind upon

The Simple System of Success

Be > Do > Have!

Can it truly be this simple?

Yes! And you'll see it all around you.

And when we see/hear any version of the verb, to be, we know we are hearing an <u>identity statement</u>.

Why do people reinforce their self-defeating beliefs by saying:

I am always late
Huh, I'm so stupid
I'm always useless at mental arithmetic

Why run those programmes? It just doesn't make any sense, does it?

If you and I asked these people to get up every morning and sit on the side of the bed for about 5 minutes. And during that time, they had to repeat, out loud, that they would catch an incurable disease.

Would they do it? They would not. And I know this for a fact as I've asked many audience members if they would.

And yet...

These same people won't take the time to programme their minds with positive suggestions about their self-worth, their likely success, and their happiness. And when I've asked why not? They reply, "Oh, that's just silly, it wouldn't work!"

And yet, they believe the negative programme would work.

Strange!

Oh well, we know what to do, don't we?

Be > Do > Have!

And here's why this is correct:

"Long-term change happens at the <u>identity</u> level"

You will have seen...

Reports of prisoners escaping from jail only to be caught within a few days.

Why were they caught so quickly and easily?

Because - they only planned to become free. They didn't plan to be free!

You will have heard about Lottery Winners who found themselves in dire straits just a few years after winning millions.

Why? They hoped to <u>become</u> rich. They never planned <u>to be</u> rich.

paid!

This is a problem for so many who are planning to change. Planning only to 'become' is setting ourselves up for failure. Planning to be a different person is how we create success.

So, if we aim to be paid at a higher level, then we must <u>be</u> the person deserving of this level of reward.

Why?

Because the reverse of my earlier-stated expression also holds true:

> ## *"People will consistently <u>do</u> who they <u>are!</u>"*
> Peter Thomson

This raises the questions:

1. Who are you?
2. What are you worth?
3. Who aren't you?

Imposter Syndrome:

We must be aware of 'Imposter Syndrome' to avoid falling into the trap. A trap that catches and hurts so many.

Imposter Syndrome is defined as the persistent <u>inability</u> to believe that one's success is <u>deserved</u> or has been <u>legitimately</u> achieved as a result of one's own efforts or skills.

We must avoid this whining at all costs!

Raising an invoice:

If we are going to raise an invoice for our time at the end of each day, then who will the invoice be sent to? If we haven't been working for a client, then we have been working for ourselves! How much will you charge yourself for your day?

Let's say you have valued your day at 1,000. If, at the end of day one of the month, you haven't invoiced for the 1,000 to a client for the day... you now have to generate 2,000 of work the next day.

If you don't raise an invoice on the second day, you will need to raise an invoice on the third day for 3,000.

If the value of a day of our time is 1,000 (and it must be far more than that!), we must be careful with the tasks we carry out during the day to make absolutely certain they are worth this value.

The Low Fee Mistake:

Here's the problem created by charging low fees.

paid!

When clients don't have enough 'skin in the game', they aren't paying at a level to feel <u>invested</u> in the process or a substantial outcome...

Then, they do not have a firm level of belief.

When their belief is low, they are unlikely to take consistent action (which many do not do...)

When they fail to take enough action, they are unlikely to achieve the increased results they said they wanted.

When that happens, they will be unhappy even with the small amount they paid

And whose reputation suffers? Yes, yours and mine.

However...

When they have 'skin in the game', they are heavily invested in their own actions and success, and their belief is firm.

When their belief is firm, they take action. When they take action consistently, their chances of success are improved. (Especially as you'll be advising them about the actions to take)

When they succeed, they are happy about how much they paid, even though it was far higher than in the previous example.

Result: Happiness! For all concerned.

Money Thoughts:

Understandably, we have some degree of cognitive dissonance about charging high fees. After all, the newspapers and media are generally full of stories about 'fat cats' and how the rich are terrible people. As a result, a climate of envy abounds.

So, let's get it clear.

When we are charging at the right level and earning high levels of income, it's not about what the money makes <u>for</u> us; it's what it makes <u>of</u> us.

"It's not what the money makes <u>for</u> us - it's what it makes <u>of</u> us!"

Peter Thomson

We step up to the plate! We give our best!

We prepare! We practice! We perform!

We become the best version of ourselves we could possibly be, knowing that someone else is perfectly prepared (and willing) to pay us to share our knowledge, experience and expertise and our take on everything we know.

As Earl Nightingale said in "Lead the Field":

paid!

"Look at these apothecary's scales. Two bowls hanging down on chains. One is labelled 'service'. One is labelled 'rewards'."

If there is not enough in the 'rewards' bowl, it is simply that we have not put enough in the service bowl.

If we wish to <u>have more</u> rewards, we must <u>give more</u> service.

"The <u>income</u> we receive is a direct reflection of the <u>outcome</u> our clients receive"

Peter Thomson

Actions:

1. Decide how much you want to be rewarded
2. Decide to be that person
3. Do the things that type of person does
4. Enjoy having the things that type of person has
5. Listen to what you say to hear how you confirm your identity. The words after "I am…" will be a clear indication of your thinking
6. Set your fee rate to only attract those who are serious about their increased success
7. Apply the following Golden Rule to all your client (and life) interactions, namely…

Don't Deal with Tossers!

What do I mean by this?

You and I know the <u>wrong</u> clients are always unhappy, even when paying the <u>right</u> price.

These are the people who moan about everything. However much we try to help them get the desired outcomes, they remain unsatisfied.

They always look to blame others rather than take the blame themselves when they are at fault. They look to take the credit even when it is not due to them.

These are the people who blame the economy, the government, the weather -almost anything (except themselves) for their lack of success. These are the people I call 'Tossers'.

Avoid dealing with 'tossers'. It makes life so much easier.

When dealing with the 'right clients', all the <u>major</u> problems become <u>minor</u>. When we are dealing with tossers, all the <u>minor</u> problems become <u>major!</u>

I don't deal with these people. And I fervently suggest you don't either.

REFRESHER 3

1. Skin in The Game

2. People will never consistently do who they aren't.

3. I bargained with life for a penny...

4. Be, Do, Have!

5. Long-term change happens at the identity level.

6. People will consistently do who they are!

7. Impostor Syndrome.

8. Raising an invoice for your time at the end of every day.

9. The Low Fee Mistake.

10. It's not what the money makes for us, it's what it makes of us!

11. The income we receive is a direct reflection of the outcome our clients receive.

12. Don't Deal With Tossers!

In the next chapter, I'm going to share with you a variety of proven pricing models to use in your 'private practice' so you can increase the level of income you receive for the incredible value you deliver.

Action Plan

Actions	Priority	When by	Done

CHAPTER FOUR

Proven Pricing Models

Let's take a look at a variety of different pricing models so you can test the ones that feel right for you. And perhaps even the ones that may feel uncomfortable at first!

Day Rate:

We've already covered a number of ideas about the value of your time. I'm sure, by now, you're at least considering testing various rates to see which level attracts those clients you love to deal with: The clients who happily pay for the value they receive from you.

Delegate Rate:

One of my clients is a successful trainer who specialises in teaching executives how to speak confidently and persuasively in public.

One of the challenges we addressed during our work together was increasing his fees. A challenge I heard about too often.

Using the idea I gave him, he increased his daily rate from an average of £1,500 a day to £4,000 a day. The £1,500 rate meant he was massively undercharging for the value he delivered and the increased results his clients invariably achieved.

Here's how:

I suggested it would be fair if he charged a Delegate Rate of £395 per day (that's not very expensive to train executives to speak in public!), with a <u>minimum</u> of 10 delegates.

He tested the idea, and it was readily accepted.

10 delegates at £395 each equal £3,950. £2,450 more per day.

Could you use this idea or a version of it? A price per X rather than a day rate? Many of my clients have used this idea and reaped their fair rewards whilst maintaining client satisfaction.

Project Rate:

Because clients are well aware of the <u>outcome value</u> of their projects - then it's often very likely they are happier paying a project rate rather than a day rate.

Proven Pricing Models

The challenge with day rates for some clients is that they have no control over how much activity and results are produced on an average day.

You may have been quoted a 'day rate' by a tradesperson. Immediately we might think, "How many days will the job take?" When we ask this question, we're met with a non-definitive answer. "About 5 days, but it might run a day or so over". An uncomfortable situation.

Example:

I was creating a personalised version of one of my multimedia programmes. (Videos, separate audios, workbooks, training, coaching, Train the Trainer) It was for a large sales division of a major company.

There were 10 modules, each approximately 20 minutes long. 300 sets of the 10 module packs were to be supplied.

The project was: writing the scripts, filming, editing, and product creation. Then training the trainers to deliver the programme. Training the managers of the 300-strong sales force.

I quoted and was paid £250,000 to complete the project. It took 10 days. I probably wouldn't have quoted (at that stage in my consulting career) £25,000 per day. The project rate was better for all involved.

paid!

The Deluxe and Double Deluxe:

Sadly, many consultants and fellow professionals leave a fortune 'on the table'! Why? Because many clients would willingly buy a deluxe version but the consultant does not offer a <u>package</u> of their services!

And there's an additional benefit. (More on this later)

Your Deluxe Package:

Let's think of your standard service as your 'premier' offering.

Then you can consider creating a higher-level offering as your Deluxe version.

Q: What could you possibly add to your premier package to increase its value to your client and increase the fee you charge?

- Could it be more time with you?
- Could it be an additional service provided by a sub-contractor
- Could it be templates
- Follow up material
- An online portal of extra content?

What else could you include?

Not filler material! But quality extras that would enhance the client's experience and the outcomes they receive.

Q: How much extra will you charge for your Deluxe version?

Your Double Deluxe:

And to the next level.

How about creating a Double Deluxe version. Now adding even greater benefits and services.

Many clients who've followed my advice on this report that the majority of clients opt for one of the deluxe versions rather than the 'premier' version.

This has produced <u>substantial</u> extra income - and extra happy clients.

The Extra Benefit:

As we will discuss in greater detail later, how having a Deluxe and Double Deluxe version of your offering provides a perfect contrast in price to your standard/premier offering.

Pricing the Deluxe Offerings:

I've consistently found my Deluxe/Double Deluxe versions were acceptable with a 5x or 10x the 'standard'/premier fee rate.

paid!

Example:

Monthly Mentoring Group members paid £500 per month.

'Take Me to Market' Members (my deluxe offering) paid £2,500 per month.

The Step-Up Model:

One way you can consider the differences between the various offerings is the following 'Step-Up' model.

Offering 1: Information
Offering 2: Information and advice
Offering 3: Information, advice and a 'done with you' service
Offering 4: Information, advice, and a 'done for you' service

Offering 1:
Information

You are simply supplying information, usually in a variety of different ways. This could be your book, online course, a webinar or seminar or even a coaching or mentoring call or course.

The client is then left to their own devices to implement your ideas and reap the rewards of their efforts.

As we know, 'the road to hell is paved with good intentions', and many clients (despite their stated willingness to take action) often do not complete the work they have to do on their own.

It's been difficult:

Over the years I've been involved in helping others to succeed, I've struggled with the idea that people do not always get the results they say they want. And the reason being - whilst the ideas work - they don't always work!

It's frustrating. And yet, some people get what they want by learning and not by applying that learning.

I know far more books are bought than read. I've just had to come to terms with this problem whilst doing my best to overcome it.

Offering 2:
Information and advice

One way to overcome the problem I've outlined is to 'package' our offerings/offers to include a level of advice on implementing the ideas we've shared.

Perhaps providing templates and extra online videos of explanation.

This has extra value for our clients and often will attract a higher price or fee.

Offering 3:
Information, advice and a 'done with you' service

In this version, we are increasing the time and service we provide to our clients. We are actively involved in helping them get the outcomes they want, albeit the client is taking the majority of the actions.

In my Private Practice - I help clients to get their books written by offering a 'done with you' service.

Spending time creating a personal plan of action, 'keeping their feet to the fire' to ensure deadlines are adhered to. And generally, 'being there for them' to answer questions and provide continued inspiration.

Offering 4:
Information, advice, and a 'done for you' service

In this version, we are becoming a member of the client's team. Taking on some of the work. In one of our lead generation services, we offer to manage the whole process for clients - creating 'first draft' articles, posting to social media, outreach to increase connections, and maintaining contact from first connection through to qualified appointments made.

And a complete 'done for you' service to whatever level the client requires.

Perhaps having read the details of these four service levels may have sparked some ideas for your future offerings/offers.

How you create your various deluxe offerings:

Use the 'Deluxing Your Offer' template

1. List everything you could supply to your clients. This might include:
    1. Additional coaching
    2. Follow-up videos
    3. Templates
    4. Guarantees
    5. Email support
    6. Telephone support
    7. Proofreading
       (if you were showing them how to create persuasive copy)
    8. Role-play sessions
    9. And whatever else you believe would add value to your client
2. Decide at which level (premier/deluxe/double deluxe) clients receive each item
3. Set the price points for each level
4. Always include 3 levels of pricing in your proposals

Deluxing Your Offer

Details *List the possible factors*	Premier	Deluxe	Double Deluxe
Notes on pricing:			
Pricing for each level:			

How to offer your Deluxe Offerings:

"Prescription before Diagnosis is Malpractice"

Tony Alessandra

This not only applies to anyone in the medical profession but also to anyone in the supply of any product or service.

Therefore, as we gather information from the prospective client, we begin to realise which level of help they need from us.

Therefore, when we explain how we can help, it makes sense to start with an overall description of the 3 levels (Premier/ Deluxe/Double Deluxe) and how each benefits the client in different ways.

I'll discuss The Contrast Principle and how to use it in much greater detail for you in Chapter 6. But for now, let's ensure that we are showing the different levels of services/ products/offerings - so we can guide the client to making the right decision.

A simple test close question along the lines of, "Which of these solutions might suit you?" will begin the process of concluding the sale.

You'll note my use of the word 'might'.

I strongly believe in using words such as: might, maybe, and perhaps. This seemingly 'soft approach' works far better than being - far too certain, far too soon! The latter approach pushes clients away rather than attracting them.

Reminder: We are NOT trying to convince someone to do anything. We are acting convincingly, and then clients will 'sell themselves' on your offering and offer. (More on this later)

I am certain you will find (if you're dealing with the 'right' clients) that many of them will opt for your Deluxe or Double Deluxe offering. In fact, I feel you'll be very pleasantly surprised by just how often this happens.

And what great news that is. We can help our clients to a far greater degree - than just a minimal intervention.

Good for them, good for us. After all:

> *"Money is the silent applause*
> *for a job well done*
> *and value delivered to others"*
>
> Peter Thomson

And with this belief firmly embedded in 'who we are', marketing, sales, client conversations, and conversions are easier, more relaxing and rewarding.

We increase our influence, our impact and (as a result) our income.

Reminder:

Proven Pricing Models

When you calculate the fee level/price of your Deluxe and Double Deluxe offerings/offers, consider 5 times to 10 times the level of your Premier offering/offer.

There are plenty of clients out there who want the top level of the service you offer. In fact, wealthy clients do NOT want to buy 'cheap' advice. Don't offer cheap!

If you only attracted, say, an average of two clients a month who were enjoying your Deluxe offerings at £2,500 per month each - that's an extra £60,000 a year. And your clients are getting greater value too.

Soft Pound/Dollar Deals:

One of the major advantages of having a well-positioned daily fee rate (or project rate) is the increased likelihood of what are known as 'soft dollar' or 'soft pound deals'.

This is where we swap our services for another service or benefit the client is able to offer.

Example:

About 20 or so years ago, I was approached by a furniture manufacturer who wanted me to help them with their marketing. I quoted my usual fee rate at that time of £5,000 per day. They were happy to go ahead. However, they suggested a soft pound deal.

So, instead of being paid the £5,000, they supplied me with a £12,000 retail price. (£5,000 cost to them) 3-piece suite.

paid!

Naturally, this had to be declared as £5,000 income. It was an excellent trade.

There are times when we consider that we need 'money' to be able to purchase something. However, it's not necessarily the money we need; it's what we will buy with the money. It's the item or service we want. And on many occasions, this can be arranged on a soft pound/dollar deal.

If our fee rate is low, then any soft pound/dollar deals we do will also be at this low exchange rate.

If our fee rate is high, then any soft pound/dollar deals we do will also be at this high exchange rate.

Creative Solutions:

Here are a couple of creative solutions when you find yourself with an opportunity to stand and speak and share your ideas. You may well be able to use these in a number of different ways.

I was discussing with a large corporate client how I could help them by training their 270 salespeople. Unfortunately, the budget did not match the amount I was proposing to charge for a series of two-day training events around the country.

Instead, I suggested that we hold a one-day event with all 270 people there and follow that with a series of one-day events around the country. As fewer days were involved, there was less investment in my time - and the contract was secured.

The Time Challenge:

As our marketing starts to work even better than before, we can find ourselves with pressure on our diaries to be able to make the days on which our clients want our help.

Because we are able to explain our ideas 'on camera', then being able to provide this 'remote help' can be very useful and work well for everyone concerned.

One client asked me to speak at 18 different events where there would be a total attendance of 7,000 of their customers. I was able to make four of the dates but not the other fourteen. I suggested I provide them with a video of my presentation (personalised with examples of all their products and services), which they could play at the events that I was not attending.

The client was happy. The attendees were happy with the content and ideas I shared (In fact, even when I was not actually there, only on screen, I was still rated as the top speaker at these events), and I was pleased with those outcomes and to be able to help my client.

REFRESHER 4

1. Proven Pricing Models.

2. Day rate.

3. Delegate rate.

4. Project rate.

5. Deluxe and Double Deluxe.

6. How to create your various deluxe offerings.

7. The Step-Up Model. Information; information and advice; information, advice and a 'done with you' service; information, advice, and a 'done for you' service.

8. Prescription before diagnosis is malpractice.

9. Soft Pound/Dollar Deals. The higher the value of your time the higher the value of the swap.

10. Creative Solutions. Filming your presentation. Group presentation with follow up one day meetings.

Action Plan

Actions	Priority	When by	Done

CHAPTER FIVE

Your Offering and Your Offer

Now let's look at the offering and the offer, how they differ and what needs to be included in each.

There is a great deal of difference between the offering and the offer.

And we must ensure those differences are clear to our clients.

After all, as Chip and Dan Heath state in their book: Decisive:

"Resistance is created through a lack of clarity"

So, let's go through this now to clarify when we are making our offerings/offers to our clients.

Important Point:

Most consultants and other professionals never give enough thought to their offerings. And end up with a weak, badly constructed set of words and phrases that are highly unlikely to engender any excitement or genuine interest in their readers' or listeners' minds.

This is your opportunity to delve deeper into <u>why</u> you are different and how you can phrase this difference to maximise your opportunities to engage those clients you love to work with.

The Offering:

The offering is:

- What your product or service <u>is</u>
- What it <u>has</u>
- What it <u>does</u>
- <u>Why</u> you have decided to deliver this product or service in this way
  (This is what separates you from others as most people never even consider explaining to their clients - 'why' they do what they do)

Example:

Even before the worldwide pandemic, I was regularly offering webinars to both market my services and deliver my content to my clients.

If, for our discussion, I consider the webinar as the offering, we can look at each of the four factors: what it is, what it has, what it does and why.

What it is:

The offering is for a one-hour webinar taking place at 10 o'clock in the morning on a Tuesday. It is being run on the Zoom platform. The name of the host and the presenter is also stated.

What it has:

The webinar has a main section where content will be shared, and there will be a coffee break and time for questions and answers.

What it does:

One of the webinars I run is to help people to write and market their informational products, starting by creating a book. The webinar is called "Your Book and Beyond".

The promise (what it does) explains my methods of:

• Gathering your knowledge, experience and expertise using a templated formula.

- How to overcome writer's block
- How to get the book laid out and printed
- How/where to get the cover designed
- How to use your book as a perfect lead magnet to attract those 'love to work with' clients.

Why this way:

As I previously mentioned, detailing why you have decided to offer your product or service in a particular way is what will separate you from the rest of the marketplace.

So, in the promotion for my webinar, 'Your Book and Beyond', I will make reference to the following:

1. This is a webinar; therefore, there is no travel time,
2. There is no travel cost,
3. No hotel costs. It can be attended from the comfort of the clients' homes or offices.
4. I have limited it to one hour, including the Q&A session, so that it does not take up a large portion of the clients' days.
5. It is being recorded, so if they are unable to attend the 'live session', they will not miss any of the ideas.
6. I've arranged it to begin at 10am, so there is time for work to be done before and plenty of time for work to be done after the webinar is finished.

Second Example: (Zoom or face-to-face meetings)

If you are offering to work with a client on a one-to-one basis, you may decide to work together remotely, i.e., on a

Your Offering and Your Offer

Zoom or Teams meeting. Or you may decide to visit their premises. Or they may come to you.

In my private practice, I work with my clients either on Zoom or they come to my home for longer sessions.

I explain the 'why' of these arrangements as follows:

So, we can maximise the time we spend together and delve deeper into each idea, so you can get the most benefit from them - would you prefer to come to see me face-to-face or meet via Zoom?

Some clients prefer to meet face-to-face. And although I love meetings and webinars via Zoom (they are so cost and time effective), I still find there's a different feeling to actual meetings.

Somehow, a greater understanding is reached, and the interplay of ideas is more engaging. Yes, the future of communication is undoubtedly through the screen or headset in virtual or mixed reality. That said - I'm also confident we'll still meet for actual coffee rather than just a virtual one in the foreseeable future!

Your offering can be made:

- On a webinar
- During a seminar
- In a proposal
- In an email
- On a webpage
- In a piece of direct mail

- In a client conversation
- Anywhere you communicate with a client or potential client

Reminder:
Your offering details what your product or service is, what it has, but it does (those are the benefits your clients' experience) and why you have decided to offer it this way.

The Offer:

Now let's look at the offer and how this differs from the offering.

The offer includes the following items:

- The price of the product or service
- The payment terms
  - How many months (or other time periods) to pay
  - How many payments
  - Any upfront payment
    - Deposit
    - Onboarding fee
      (so few people even consider charging an onboarding fee and leave thousands 'on the table')
  - Any back-end payment
    - Follow-up materials
    - Offboarding (unusual, but very useful for your clients and you)

- A contingency or commission payment
- Bonuses being offered and the value of those bonuses
- Scarcity
  - Bonuses are only available until a specific date or until a certain number have been taken
  - Time – how much time you are prepared to offer for working with clients
  - Availability – if your diary is full of other work, then it would make sense to explain this to a potential client so they realise you are a scarce resource and other clients are using your services.
  - Price – only available at this price for a certain number of buyers or until a specific date.
- The Call to Action (CTA) or the Call to Value (CTV)

Let's look at each of these and dive into more detail to maximise the conversion rate of any offering and offer we make.

Product/Service Pricing:

We have already discussed several ideas for pricing your products and services. I urge you to refer back to that list and test different methods, ideas, and prices in your particular marketplace.

In chapter 6, we go through, in some detail, how to use The Contrast Principle and why <u>everything</u> you say and do before you quote your price is critically important to the client's feelings about your charges.

paid!

Payment Terms:

I'm aware of numerous tests that have been carried out, which indicate how much easier it is to sell a product or service when payment terms are offered.

My own experiences also show far more sales are made when clients are able to pay over a period of time.

Example:

In one of my programmes, I ran a one-day course and, having given immense value, went on to offer a 3-day course. On the 3-day course, having given further value, I offered a 12-month mentoring programme.

On the one-day course, when I offered payment terms for the 3-day course, sales were substantially higher.

It also seems that offering 3 payments rather than 2 payments increases sales.

There is an important point here concerning cash flow:

If we offer 3 monthly payments, we receive the money in just 2 months.

One payment is made at the point of signing, one payment is made one month later, and one payment is made a further month later. All monies received in 2 months.

Similarly, if we want to extend the payment terms for our clients, we can offer a 4-month payment plan where we receive the money in 3 months.

Upfront Payments:

Having discussed the idea of being paid for the value they deliver with a number of consultants and coaches, I realised many of them were <u>not</u> charging for the work they were doing prior to the first delivery meeting with the client.

Often, this was quite a substantial amount of work.

For example:

One consultant told me that if she had to charge for the work, she was doing prior to the first meeting, she would have wanted to raise an invoice for £3,000. I asked her why she wasn't raising the invoice, and she struggled to come up with a reply!

I suggested she start charging it. At first, she was somewhat cautious about asking for the full £3,000 and started by asking for £1,000.

She found her clients gladly agreed when they realised the amount of work, she was doing for them. Later she increased that fee to £3,000.

paid!

Deposit:

The idea of charging a deposit before the main payments is another way of being rightfully rewarded for the work we do.

For example:

"Make the First Sale an Easy Sale"
Peter Thomson

I created the following when I was running the one-day seminars and offering the 3-day programme with a 3-part payment plan.

For a £1,995 course, instead of offering a payment plan of 3 payments of £667, I offered this:

- First payment (on the day) - £100

- Second payment - 1 month later £632

- Third payment - 1 month later £632

- Fourth payment - 1 month later £632

In this way, I was able to make the first payment very small but still gain a commitment that the client would attend the course and make the payments. This worked far better than simply offering three payments of £667.

I subtracted £100 from the £1,995 and divided the balance (£1,895) by 3, giving 3 payments of £632.

I tested another version of - £200 first payment (the joining fee) and then 3 payments of £598

Here are a number of ways in which you can ethically and rightfully charge a "deposit".

You can change the terminology to suit your style, our business, and the field in which you operate.

Onboarding fee:

If you're offering a subscription or membership programme, either as a standalone offering or as part of your main offering, it is very reasonable to ask for an onboarding fee on many occasions.

There will be actions you or your colleagues have to take, costs to be paid, and time to be spent.

And - if you have regularly asked for and been paid this onboarding fee, then you have the opportunity, in the future, to waive the fee to increase signups.

This is not the same as those who say they are waiving a fee they have never charged!

Different names you can use for these initial payments:

paid!

- Deposit
- Joining fee
- Enrolment fee
- Onboarding fee
- Research free
- Admission
- Initiation
- Booking fee
- Filing fee
- Signing up fee
- Entrance fee
- Inception fee
- Onset fee

- Diagnostics fee
- Business scan
- Market scan
- Health check
- Wealth check
- Welcome pack
- Concierge fee
- Induction fee
- Application fee
- Qualification fee
- Registration fee
- Briefing fee
- Acceptance fee

The Financial Impact:

By way of example, let's imagine that we onboard 20 new clients every year into our private practice.

If you charge an onboarding fee of £1,000 for each client, that's an additional bottom-line profit of £20,000 per annum.

If you are running a membership programme where you meet with the members for, say, one day a month - and you charge an onboarding/joining fee of £200, and you have 20 members, then that's an additional income of £4,000 for each cohort.

If you are running a subscription programme with 200 subscribers paying, say, £50 a month and you charge a joining fee of the equivalent of one month's subscription (£50), that's an additional £10,000 of income.

All of these payments are fair and reasonable and go straight to your bottom-line profit.

Back-End Payments:

Now let's look at the potential for back-end payments.

Follow-Up Materials:

You and I know the biggest challenge in training/exchanging ideas is the retention of the information by either delegates or clients.

Therefore, we must provide follow-up material so we can review the ideas, methods, and systems we shared.

This follow-up material can be audio, video, paper-based, online, templates, coaching, additional training of managers or training department personnel.

In fact, whatever you believe will give your clients the best possible opportunity of both retaining the ideas you shared and using those ideas to gain the additional results they came to you for in the first place.

The Money:

> *"It's not what it makes <u>for</u> you,*
> *it's what it makes <u>of</u> you"*
>
> Peter Thomson

Example:

When I started in the 'helping business', I focused on training salespeople to be more successful. These salespeople were working in a corporate environment.

Retention of information is the key to the success of any training because, without retention, ideas cannot be used.

Therefore, I knew I had to provide 'back up material' for both the salespeople and their managers so the ideas could be revisited and checked that the methods were being used and producing increased results.

Action is the Key!

I created a 30-part audio programme and was only prepared to provide the training to my clients if they agreed that <u>each member</u> of the sales team that I was training received their own personal copy of this programme. It was called 'Action is the Key'.

Even back then, many years ago, I charged £300 per set; therefore, for every team of 20 I trained, I received an additional £6,000 in income.

The income isn't the point...

You and I want to ensure our clients are getting what they want - increased results!

And I know from personal experience and from the experiences of my own clients (consultants and coaches) that clients are very happy to pay for follow-up material that helps them get their desired results.

Offboarding:

Now, I know this sounds like a bit of a strange expression. We've already looked at onboarding, but arranging appropriate offboarding offers allows us to add value and additional income.

Example: 1>3>6 Process

One way you can help your clients to achieve the outcomes they want, at the level of investment they wish to make in themselves, is my 1>3>6 process.

You start by offering a one-hour free webinar in the marketplace and to your own list.

On this webinar, you deliver an amazing amount of value and offer people to join you for a three or four-week programme (at an hour and a half to 2 hours per week) for a relatively low price.

paid!

It might be that 200 people will attend the one-hour free webinar, and then 100 - 120 of those people will pay a £100 fee for the three or four-week programme.

On this three-week programme, again, you will deliver massive value and make an offering for a six-month programme at approximately £500 per month per person. Let's say that 20 people or more will take up the six-month programme offer.

We can see how this works financially.

From the one-hour webinar, there is no income.
Then, income from the three-week programme is between £10,000 and £12,000.
From the six-month programme, the income is £60,000 plus.
Now, here's where the Offboarding offer comes in.

The way I do it is this:

Because I run a monthly membership programme called The Achievers Club (monthly subscription is £97) –I include this in the offering for the six-month programme.

What would typically happen at the end of a six-month programme, as I've described it?

Nothing!

It's the end of the arrangement. It's the end of the payments.

However, because I have included membership of The Achievers Club for the six months of the training programme;

and because I've arranged to take the monthly payments in two parts:

Payment 1 -the monthly training fee of £451
Payment 2 -The Achievers Club monthly subscription of £49

Then, at the end of the six months, clients <u>gladly continue</u> with their membership of The Achievers Club.

In other words, they have been offboarded into The Achievers Club. That's a monthly payment of £49 plus taxes.

So, if there were 20 clients in the six-month programme, collectively, they are now paying £980 per month on an ongoing basis.

As you can see, with a series of 1>3>6 webinars, increasing membership of a membership club or subscription programme and the monthly income it produces may not take too long.

How can you use this 'Offboarding' idea?

Ongoing Subscription or Membership fees:

What a wonderful feeling it is to start looking at your bank records every month and seeing a stream of monthly payments in the receipts column. Yes!

paid!

We already discussed the idea of having a follow-up programme to help your clients both remember the ideas you share with them and put them into practice.

Now let's look at the ideas of subscription and membership.

Subscription Programme:

You might consider running a subscription programme where you provide (in a variety of different formats) ongoing information to help your clients solve the problems they encounter and capitalise on the opportunities that come their way.

Possibilities:
- A monthly webinar
- A series of email training
- An online video
- Templates and workbooks

The choices are almost endless.

Let's imagine it takes one year for you to achieve a subscriber base of 100 Members. Perhaps they are paying £50 a month. And if they stay for the following year, this could generate an income of £60,000 (£5,000 a month).

Let's say you've decided to charge £20 a month and provide the information in one of the ways I've previously suggested. At this lower rate, it might be possible to gain more subscribers.

Perhaps after one year, you will be able to gain 200 subscribers who are paying £20 a month. That's £4,000 a month. That's £48,000 a year.

Important note:

If you decide to run a subscription programme where you provide monthly information, then I urge you to start all new subscribers with them receiving the <u>current monthly issue</u>. This will make your administration far easier.

If it's necessary for your clients to go through your information in a sequence, then we can consider this as a '<u>continuity programme</u>' rather than a subscription programme. In this case, you'll have everyone starting at Issue #1

I've been running subscription programmes for over 30 years. They are an excellent way of sharing our ideas with our clients, providing excellent value at a very affordable price -and these programmes are very profitable.

I've also found many of my private clients have come from people who started as subscribers or members of my monthly audio newsletter or members of my monthly webinar series.

Membership Programme:

Another way of providing our information and methods is by way of a monthly membership programme. This could be like a mastermind group.

paid!

Here are a number of different versions I've run over a number of years - perhaps you might consider doing the same.

Monthly Mentoring Group:

I've referred to my monthly mentoring groups in previous sections. Here's a bit more detail for you. I gained members by running a one-day event, offering a three-day event at the seminar, and then offering membership in the mentoring group at the three-day event.

Members paid (on average) £500 per month. It was a one-year programme with a quarterly group backend.

Let's look at the finances. If you gained, say, 20 members who are paying £500 per month, that's £10,000 per month, which equals £120,000 per year.

If you were able to put together a group of, say, 10 people who are paying £500 per month, that equates to £60,000. You may decide that it's not limited to a one-year programme, but it's ongoing.

The 100+ Club:

I ran this club for five years. It was an ongoing Membership programme. It averaged 40 members. We met for two days every quarter, and the monthly membership fee was £395.

You can see that the monthly income was around £15,000. (£180,000 per annum).

Not only was it an ideal setting in which I was able to share my ideas, but it was also a great deal of fun, and the members achieved some remarkable results. And it was profitable.

The Adventurers

As I mentioned earlier, I currently run a quarterly mentoring group called: The Adventurers, where we meet for two days every quarter and have dinner together on the middle night.

When I run a quarterly programme, I also meet with the members in the intervening months - on a webinar.

You could run the whole programme online or offline; it's a choice.

How can you use this idea? What might it be worth?

Contingency or Commission Payment:

As we briefly discussed before, it is possible to provide our services based on a contingency (i.e., the client gets the result they were looking for - before we get paid) or a commission payment where we take a percentage on the increased sales or increase profits the client achieves as a result of using our ideas.

paid!

We could also offer a part fee/part commission arrangement where we take a reduced fee and then commission on increased sales or increased profits.

Warning:

We need to be careful to take a percentage of turnover rather than a percentage of profit.

Here's why...

We will not be in control as to how much expense is incurred in the business to be deducted from the turnover to produce the profit figure.

Taking a lower turnover percentage than a higher profit percentage is far better. This is because the turnover figure has to be shown in a number of different areas, particularly on a tax return (VAT) or in the company accounts.

Whilst the turnover figure can be incorrect, it is far less likely to be so than the profit figure, where deductions are out of our hands.

I'm not suggesting that a client would cheat, No! Just being cautious.

Second Warning:

Over time you are bound to be approached with a request to undertake joint venture deals. And whilst this can look very attractive and sometimes can be very profitable, there is an important point I'd like to make.

Let's say that a client suggests you use your marketing expertise to help them market their product/service and offer you 20% – 50% on sales or profits.

If we compare this to you spending the same amount of time marketing and selling your products and services, we immediately realise that you get 100% of the profits for those sales.

There needs to be something different in the proposed joint-venture arrangement to make us consider spending time in somebody else's business rather than spending time on our own business.

No, this is not to say that all joint-venture opportunities should be avoided. But they need to be looked at carefully to ensure that we're not spending time (irreplaceable) that could be spent for 100% of the turnover and profits in our own hands.

Bonuses and their Value:

A major part of creating a desire within the 'offer' stage is by adding bonuses.

Important Point:

We must avoid the mistake made by so many people when they state a particular bonus is FREE. Unless we give the bonus a value before saying, 'It's Free', then we imply it was always free.

However, we need to be careful because any 'false' values will destroy the credibility of both us and our offering/offers.

Bonus Suggestions:

1. Additional resources such as online materials (video/audio/templates)
2. Additional time with you
3. Valuable extras provided by others for your clients.
4. Discount vouchers for other products and services provided by you or by other suppliers.
5. Previous recordings of webinars or seminars.
6. And anything else you feel your client will value and will add benefits to them.

Scarcity:

We discussed scarcity in some depth in Chapter 1, so I would refer you back to that section to ensure you include appropriate scarcity within the offer part of your offering/offer.

You may only make the bonuses available until a specific time/date or a certain number has been taken.

You are a scarce resource!

And it makes sense (and has a persuasive impact) for clients and potential clients to realise this fact.

Price can also be scarce if you have decided to only offer the product or service at a certain price for a certain period or until a certain number of them have been purchased.

Of all the influential factors we can bring into play - scarcity is the one that creates immediate action. And because it is so powerful, we need to be careful with its use. Any hint of disingenuousness will have clients 'running for the hills'.

The Call to Action / The Call to Value:

And the final part of the 'offer section' is the call to action.

On many websites and their order pages, you have seen the commonly used word on 'call to action' buttons. The word used is 'Submit'. What a terrible expression to use when there are so many other persuasive and positive words or phrases.

So, when crafting your 'call to action', consider the context in which it will be used.
For example, will it be in writing throughout an email? Will it be underneath the detail boxes on your website when you've asked somebody for their information so they can receive your free report?
Will it be spoken at the end of your offering/offer on a webinar or seminar? Will it be at the end of a promotional video?

paid!

Examples of Calls to Action:

Yes, Peter, please send me my copy of the seven BIG mistakes report.

Note the change of possessive pronoun. Send me <u>my</u> copy...

It is no longer <u>my</u> report (in the sense of me the author) or <u>the</u> report (neutral position); it is now the <u>reader's</u> report.

- Count me in
- Add to cart
- Buy now
- Download now
- Learn more
- Start here

Examples of Calls to Value:

I love the idea of 'calls to value' from Joanna Weibe of Copyhackers. It's a very clever idea.

We complete the sentences in the following examples to craft a' call to value'.

I want to...
I want you to help me to...

Your Offering and Your Offer

Examples:

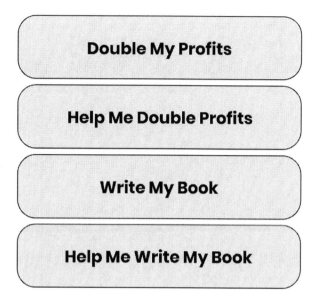

Suggestion:

If you have any questions about the offering and offer, please contact me at: success@peterthomson.com

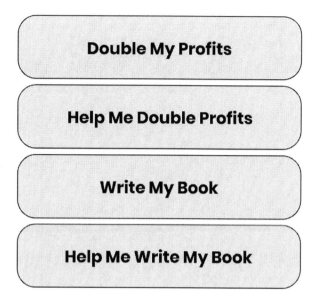

REFRESHER 5

1. Your Offering and Your Offer

2. Resistance is created through a lack of clarity.

3. The Offering. What it is, what it has, what it does, and why are you have decided to deliver it in this way.

4. The Offer. The price, the payment terms, upfront payment, on boarding fee, back in payments, contingency payments, off boarding, bonuses, scarcity, availability, call to action all the call to value.

5. Subscription and Membership Programs.

In the next chapter I'll share with you one of the most important ideas on how you get rightfully rewarded for the difference you make.

If there was one way of positioning your fees, which has been proven to work time and again in the real world, it would be The Contrast Principle. Let's dive into it now.

Action Plan

Actions	Priority	When by	Done

CHAPTER SIX

The Contrast Principle

If I had to share my thoughts with anyone about the most powerful idea in positioning the price of our products or our fees, then it would be - The Contrast Principle.

Having used this idea for over 50 years in business, I'm convinced that price objections more easily follow when contrast is <u>not</u> created.

So what is The Contrast Principle?

I can most easily demonstrate this for you by explaining a real-world example.

Some years ago, I discussed training a major company's 300-strong sales team. I suggested to them, rather than a physical training course, which would take the sales team members 'off the road' - I would create a personalised ten-part programme using some of the modules in my Accelerated Business Growth System.

paid!

(The ABGS programme included: DVDs, CDs, workbooks, templates and checklists)

This idea received a positive response, and now the price had to be discussed.

Here's how the conversation went:

Me: How many salespeople do you have?
Client: We have 300 salespeople.
Me: And what might you be losing in sales (for whatever reason) per person per month? Would that be £10,000 a month, £1,000 a month, or £2,000 a month?
Client: It must be at least £2,000 a month
Me: And how long has this situation been going on? Is it five years, one year, or two years?
Client: It's probably about two years
Me: Let's look at what that's cost you.
Me: 300 salespeople lost £2,000 per month each, in sales equals £600,000. Multiplied by 12 equals £7.2 million. Multiplied by two years equals £14.4 million. Does that sound about right?
Client: I've never thought about it that way, but yes, it is that astonishing amount.
Me: As the sales manager, do you usually make a commission on the sales of your sales team?
Client: Yes, I do.
Me: Oh! In that case, how much money do you feel (change of language to kinaesthetic - feel) you have missed over the last two years?
Client: I hate to think.
Me: Is your sales team fairly stable. In the sense that there is a low churn rate?

Client: Yes, pretty stable.

Me: Well, in that case, if you did nothing different for the next year, there is a possibility you would lose another £7.2 million in sales, is that right?

Client: Yes, that's more than likely

Me: I have some good news. (smiling) It's not going to cost £7.2 million to solve this problem.

Result: The client was very happy to pay £250,000 for me to create a 10-module training pack where each salesperson in their team (300 of them) received a copy. This included audio, video and paper-based solutions. I also trained members of the training department on how to deliver the material and trained the management team on how to coach the sales team members.

Additional benefit: When another company saw what had happened, they asked me to create a seven-module pack for their 100-strong sales team at a fee of £125,000.

You can clearly see the idea of The Contrast Principle in play in the conversation. You realise I have only included the essential elements of the conversation to demonstrate how the contrast was created.

Important Note:

This is NOT creating a contrast to the fees of other consultants or suppliers - no! This creates a contrast to the current or future state of the client. For clarity:

*"We sell price, based on
the contrast between
the <u>financial</u> and <u>emotional</u> impact of
the problem compared to the price of
(or investment in) our solution"*

Peter Thomson

And to be able to do this, we must go back to the idea of:
Important:

*"Selling takes place in
the gathering stage as people
sell themselves in their answers
to your well-crafted questions"*

Peter Thomson

Here's why it is essential to create the contrast:

*"Without contrast, everything sounds
expensive, or cheap!"*

Peter Thomson

And the challenge is - we do <u>not</u> know which one it is.

Therefore, we have to take control of the financial thinking of our prospective client (or client) in a non-manipulative way to ensure they realise <u>the financial downsides</u> of their current situation and the potential <u>financial upsides</u> of our solution.

Here's a way to remember we must use The Contrast Principle in every single client interaction we ever have when talking about price.

This can be in an email, on a webpage, in a proposal, in a seminar, on a webinar, in a video, on a social media post; basically, in any and every situation where price is mentioned.

Here's why:

"It's what you <u>say</u> before you <u>say</u> what you mean to <u>say</u>, that makes the difference."

"It's what you <u>do</u> before you <u>do</u> what you mean to <u>do</u> that also makes the difference."

And when we put these two together:

*"It's what you say and do,
before you say and do,
what you really mean to say and do,
that really makes a difference!"*
Peter Thomson

So, how are we going to create this contrast?

We can do it in the way I described in my conversation with the client about training a 300-person sales team, or rather than focus on the downsides (which is what I was doing in that conversation), we focus on the upsides.

I call this: Future First, Present Next!

Let me explain:

This is very powerful when dealing with an individual client. I found, and I'm sure you've found the same, that some people can exaggerate when asked to answer how much money they make or what their turnover is. Have you also experienced this?

So, the way in which I've altered my 'gathering' was - future first, present next.

Client Conversation Gathering Document

I've included a copy of my 'Client Conversation Gathering Document' and urge you to create your own version of this as it gives us so much control in the gathering part of the converstion.

Client Conversation

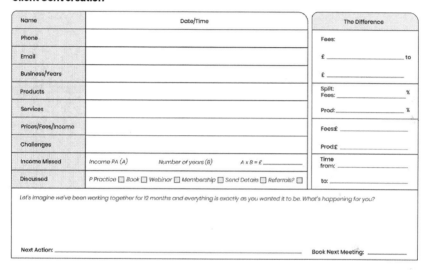

Name	Date/Time		The Difference
Phone			Fees:
Email			£ _____ to
Business/Years			£ _____
Products			Split: Fees: _____ %
Services			Prod: _____ %
Prices/Fees/Income			Fees:£ _____
Challenges			Prod:£ _____
Income Missed	Income PA (A) _____ Number of years (B) _____ A x B = £ _____		Time from: _____
Discussed	P.Practice ☐ Book ☐ Webinar ☐ Membership ☐ Send Details ☐ Referrals? ☐		to: _____
Let's imagine we've been working together for 12 months and everything is exactly as you wanted it to be. What's happening for you?			
Next Action: _____			Book Next Meeting: _____

As you can see, there are a variety of boxes to be completed as we gather information from the prospective client. If we're aiming to help a client increase their turnover, profits and personal income, then naturally, we'll need to know what's currently happening.

However, this is where a problem can occur.

When I've asked a prospective client how much they are currently turning over, I've often felt they have slightly exaggerated the number.

paid!

To counteract this problem, this is what I do...

I've used this question for at least 40 years, if not longer, and it's proved its worth time and time again.

"Let's imagine (name) and I have been working together for 12 months. It's been going well. We've enjoyed it. We've had fun with serious intent. So here we are, 12 months down the road. Tell me, how much monthly turnover are you now enjoying (in 12 months' time)?

If the client does not give me a number quickly, I will suggest some. Like this: "Would that be £50,000 a month? £15,000 a month? £25,000 a month?" And I know from experience that suggesting appropriate numbers will help the client to decide how much they want their turnover to be.

You'll note the number sequence was high/low/middle.

I will suggest numbers relevant to the client and their circumstances from the research I carried out before the meeting, or information I've gathered during the conversation prior to this point.

Let's say the client said £25,000 a month in 12 months' time.

Then I would ask, "And how does that compare to today?" They might say, "That's an increase of £15,000 a month".

Doing it this way, I found the client gives me the gap between the intended turnover per month in 12 months' time; and the current monthly turnover.

The Contrast Principle

This 'Gap Number' (in the above example, £180,000 extra in a year) is critically important to creating the contrast between where they wish to be - and where they are now. And it's needed to position our fees appropriately for us to help them get this increased financial result.

The conversation would continue:

"So, you'd like me to help you to increase your turnover by £180,000 a year (12 times £15,000), is that right?" The client will say, "Yes". There is no other logical choice. I'm using the figures they gave me and then simply asking for confirmation they wish to achieve this.

I might continue asking, "And how many more years are you aiming to be in business?" And I'll wait for the answer. Let's say the client replies, "At least 10 more years".

I will continue with the following:

"So, £180,000 a year for at least 10 more years is at least £1.8 million, and that's not even allowing for the increases per year, over those 10 years."

"Excellent, now I know what we must focus on to get you this additional turnover and the profits and income this can generate for you".

You can clearly see how this 'Future First Present Next' system positions and contrasts the fees you will quote to help your client get the desired outcomes.

Manipulation:

This is an appropriate time to talk about manipulation. I'm often asked about it.

"Manipulation is the intent of the user"

So it is with any communication device. Yes, they can be used manipulatively. You know I do <u>not</u> suggest this in any way. However, they can also be used with integrity to help our clients achieve desired outcomes.

Price Objections:

Over the years of helping many consultants and other professionals to be rightfully rewarded for the differences they make, I've often been asked about 'handling price objections'.

And here's my 'take 'on the whole idea of objections:

Important:

Most objections (most, not all) are <u>created by what we didn't do or didn't say earlier in the conversation;</u> rather than what we did say or did do just before the point at which the objection was raised.

The Contrast Principle

The 11 reasons why Price Objections occur:

1. Forgetting to use The Contrast Principle.
2. Not finding out what the client really wants to achieve.
3. Not finding out the true value of that outcome to them.
4. Not using a Client Conversation Gathering Document.
5. Not positioning ourselves as the natural and logical choice to help them on their journey.

(And not being an author of our own business book)

6. Not using an agenda.
7. Not having Deluxe or Double Deluxe versions of our offerings.
8. Not having a planned, prepared and practised opening to the conversation.
9. Jumping to the 'Presentation Stage' before gathering sufficient information to establish whether we are able to help the client.
10. Not being confident when we state our fees.
11. And the reverse problem: quoting a fee rate that is far too low compared to the value we can deliver and the outcome the client will experience. This will often prompt the client to look for other suppliers or solutions. (Hence the expression: Unbelievably cheap).

Building Our Price Quoting Muscles:

Let's start this session together with a focused quote:

> *"Amateurs practice till they get it right, professionals practice till they cannot get it wrong!"*

And isn't that so true?

Now, the last thing we want to do is to practice when we are in a conversation with a potential client. Far better to practice with a colleague or friend or even in the mirror.

Here is a very simple way to build our 'price quoting muscles'.

- Describe to a friend or colleague the major benefits they will get if they engage you to do what you do.
- When they fully understand your offering, ask them to ask you, "And how much will that cost?"
- You reply with your normal fee rate.

Now we will do it differently...

Again, you will describe to your friend or colleague the benefits they will get if they engage you to do what you do. However, this time you are going to quote 5 times your normal rate when they ask you, "And how much would that cost?"

The Contrast Principle

I'm fairly certain you will be more enthusiastic in the description of what you do and the benefits they receive (knowing you're going to be quoting 5 times your normal price). Is that true?

Okay, do that exercise. How does it feel quoting 5 times your normal rate?

Now we are going to take it up a level...

I'd like you to do the whole exercise again. However, when your friend or colleague asks you, "And how much will that cost?" you will reply <u>with a figure 10 times your normal rate</u>.

Am I right in thinking you need to demonstrate even greater clarity about what you're going to do for your client and be even more specific and descriptive with the benefits they will receive not only in the short term but in the medium and long-term as well?

If this is true, and I know from personal experience of having run this exercise with so many people, that it is true, just imagine how different this will be.

Questions:

How do you feel about quoting 10 times your normal rate? Does it feel a little awkward, perhaps a bit embarrassing, out of the box?

Okay, now for the fourth part of this exercise:

And this time, I would like you to describe your offering in the same enthusiastic way you used knowing you were going to quote 10 times your usual rate; however, this time, despite this powerful, passionate, and persuasive description, you're going to go back to quoting your standard fee. Yes, your standard fee!

Here's what others have said to me at the end of this exercise.

- Huh, I won't be quoting that low fee for all this value and benefit I'm delivering!
- My usual fee is far too low.
- I'm going to change it now.
- I've been undercharging for years.

Are any of these words resonating with you? Do you now feel that perhaps the fee you've been charging is far too low for the value and benefit you're delivering?

Well, if you do...

Maybe now is the time to re-evaluate your fees and charges.

This 'contrast' exercise came from two experiences.

The first was driving down the motorway at around 70 miles an hour and then pulling off into a minor road where the speed limit was only 30 miles an hour. Having left the motorway, I slowed down to what I thought was 30 miles an hour. However, I still did 45 miles an hour when I looked at the speedometer. I'm sure you've had this happen.

The second occasion was in the days when I was playing golf. And I saw an advert for a heavier-than-normal practice golf club. It was the same idea as holding three clubs and swinging with them. Once I swung the heavy club (or the three clubs together), my normal club produced a much faster swing speed.

You can see how these two experiences led to the 'Contrast' 10 times the price exercise.

I've had many clients report back to me how easy it was for them to change their fees once they've been through this exercise and realised how much value they delivered, and the value of that value to their clients.

The School of Life book, 'Why We Hate Cheap Things', has a wonderful quote. This brings home why we must charge the 'right' fees.

"A reduction in our esteem for an experience follows a reduction in the cost of obtaining it"

NOTE:
This 'reduction' might be a reaction to our <u>expectation</u> of the cost, not an actual reduction.

Testing Your Price:

Over the years, I've asked many consultants, coaches and various other professionals, "When was the last time you tested your price?" I've also asked, "When was the last time you raised your price?"

Both questions usually receive answers of, "Ugh, some years ago!"

I suggested that perhaps now is the time for testing to determine at what fee rate or price the maximum number of clients is engaged.

I'm sure you've had a situation in your life, as I've had in mine when a price or fee quoted by a supplier or tradesperson felt too low and destroyed our feelings about the provider and the certainty of the outcome we were seeking.

It's necessary to test different prices and different offerings, different offers to find out what works better/best.

Once we have a model that's working, that's called 'The Control '. In future, we want to test 'against the control' to see if a new version, perhaps even a higher price, produces better results.

Naturally, if you do not have a regular stream of qualified leads with whom you can test your offerings and offers, it can be difficult to 'take the risk' you might not get the client.

Later, I'll explain my thoughts on creating a stream of qualified leads so you can have the opportunity to carry out the tests I've suggested.

Practice Makes Permanent:

An often-heard expression is, "Practice Makes <u>Perfect</u>"; whilst this has some validity, it's not strictly accurate. Here's why:

Some years ago, I used to play golf. I was very keen, playing three times a week and practising regularly. Then, unfortunately, I had a problem with my back, which meant I was unable to play for six months. On my return, I realised I hadn't missed my golf as much as I'd anticipated, so I decided to stop playing. In my playing days, my handicap was 11, which was not too bad!

As a regular driving range and practice area attendee, I would see fellow golfers practising like crazy!

The majority were practising without any plan of any sort or any idea of what they were really trying to achieve. Instead, they were working on the misguided thought process that - practice makes perfect!

In fact, practice makes it <u>permanent</u>. Only perfect practice makes <u>perfect and permanent</u>.

Those golfers whacking balls down the range, slicing them most of the time, were 'locking in their slice'. No surprise, on the course, I saw them demonstrating the results of their perfect practice, their regular slice!

You and I know differently.

When we practice, we must practice 'for real'.

We must imagine conversing with the client and describing all the features, benefits, and advantages of our offering with passion, persuasion, and purpose...

And then detail our offer, the price, the payment terms, and the call to action or value as though we were in a real conversation with a client.

As I previously mentioned, we can carry out this exercise with a friend or colleague, or even a best friend, the 'one looking back from the glass [mirror].'

As I stated at the beginning of the chapter:

> *"Amateurs practice till they get it right, professionals practice till they cannot get it wrong!"*

Suggestion:

When planning a client meeting and preparing all the necessary documentation, including time to practice those parts of the conversation that are critical to your success.

Think of this idea in the following way:

If the client you're about to see was the client who will be responsible for all your income for the next 10 years, then how well prepared, researched, and practised, would you be?

We both know the answer.

REFRESHER 6

1. The Contrast Principal.

2. We sell price based on the contrast between the financial and emotional impact of the problem compared to the price or investment in our solution.

3. Without contrast everything sounds expensive, or cheap!

4. We must take control of the client's financial thinking.

5. It's what you say before you say what you mean to say.

6. Client Conversation Gathering Document. Create this and use it for every client meeting.

7. Price Objections. Most objections are created by what we don't say earlier in the conversation rather than what we do you say just prior to mentioning the price.

8. Amateurs practice till they get it right, professionals practice till they cannot get it wrong.

9. Strengthening our pricing quoting muscles. Practice at 10 times the price.

10. Testing your prices.

11. Practice Makes Permanent. Perfect practice makes perfect and permanent.

In the next chapter, I'll go through the four golden questions of business growth. And give you a variety of answers to these questions. I'm sure you'll not only use them in your business; you'll also share them with your clients.

What a difference they can make!

The Contrast Principle

Action Plan

Actions	Priority	When by	Done

Get Your FREE Copy

Because you're a reader of **paid!**

You're entitled to your FREE copy of the essential

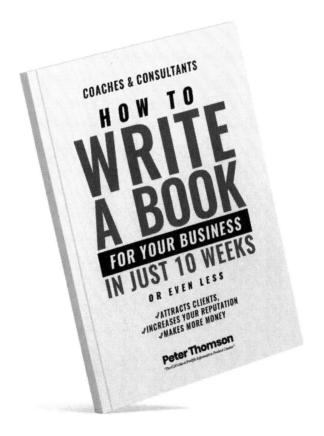

Simply go to:

www.thepaidbook.com/downloads

CHAPTER SEVEN

The Four Questions of Business Growth

Over the course of my business life, I've been very fortunate to meet some very successful and clever people. Having decided to launch and run an <u>audio</u> newsletter called, The Achievers Edge (the first of its kind in the world), I included an interview with a successful person in every month's issue.

Over the years, I've interviewed 174 people and had one-to-one conversations where I learnt so many brilliant ideas.

A friend of mine, David Hughes, the then managing director of Nightingale Conant in the United Kingdom, told me about a seminar he'd been to in Los Angeles. The seminar presenter was Jay Abraham, the famous marketeer.

David suggested I go. I went. And heard from Jay the three key questions of business growth. Later, I became friends

paid!

with Ted Nicholas, one of, if not the most successful self-published authors and a marketing genius responsible for billions of dollars of sales by his clients. Ted also explained the three key questions of business growth and gave me numerous answers to those questions.

I also interviewed Paul Dunn. Another top marketer and businessman now involved in the worldwide charity: B1G1. He also explained the four business growth questions to me.

Here are the four questions:

1. How do you increase the number of customers?
2. How do you increase the average order value?
3. How do you increase the average order frequency?
4. How do you increase the average retention rate?

Simple questions, but the answers are the solutions to all our business growth problems. Over the years, I've collected over 160+ answers to question #1, 120+ answers to question #2, 20+ answers to question #3 and 50+ answers to question #4.

Let me go through the maths of the four questions and give you a number of answers you can work with immediately, so you can increase your turnover, profits and personal income.

If you'd like the complete lists of answers for the four questions, just pop over to:
www.thepaidbook.com/downloads

The Maths:

Here is the explanation for the table below:

A/O/V = average order value; A/O/F = average order frequency

	Customers	A/O/V	A/O/F	Turnover
1	100	100	2	20,000
2	110	100	2	22,000
3	110	110	2.2	26,620
4	120	120	2.2	31,680
5				
6				

On line #1, you can see we are examining an example business' accounts and note they have 100 customers who are spending an average of £100: twice in the period under examination.

100 customers multiplied by £100 × 2 = £20,000.

This is the turnover of the business:

The number of customers multiplied by how much they spend, each time they spend it, multiplied by how often they spend the amount.

Now let's look at how we can increase the turnover and profits of an example business.

paid!

Let's say we are able to increase the number of customers by 10%.

You can now see, on line 2, I have increased the number of customers to 110.

So, the turnover will now increase by 10%. 110 customers multiplied by £100 average order value multiplied by two (the average order frequency) equals £22,000. Linear growth.

This is what most people do. They concentrate only on increasing the number of customers.

Naturally, we must have consistent marketing and sales activity, bringing more customers or clients to the top of the marketing funnel. Because we will lose some as time goes by.

Some will move. Some will go out of business. Some will merge. Sometimes, our main contact in a client company leaves to go to another company, and we lose the connection.

However, there is a better way to grow...

Rather than concentrating on only increasing the number of customers (necessary though this is), we will also focus on increasing the average order value and - increasing the average order frequency.

You can see what happens in line 3.

Now the business has 110 customers spending £110 each time they spend and spending this amount 2.2 times in the period under examination. The turnover has increased to £26,620. This is an increase of 33.1% as we are now gaining the extra amount through the multiplying effect of the three factors.

In line 4, you can see I've increased the number of customers by 20%, average order value by 20% and average order frequency by just 10%.

The turnover has now increased to £31,680, an increase in profits of £11,680. That's a 58% increase.

"Turnover is Vanity, Profit is Sanity, Cash is Reality!"

Let's look at the potential profit in these increases. First, in many companies adding 10% to the number of customers, the average order value and the average order frequency will <u>not</u> involve them in any increase in the number of staff, larger premises, increased marketing budgets, or any other of the basic costs of any business.

Yes, there may be a slight increase to allow for the cost of providing a product or service. However, as a consultant or other professional where the major cost is our time, there is no additional cost.

Therefore, the increased £6,620 on line three or the increase of £11,680 on line 4 are all pure profit! So, when we look at increases; rather than the increase at the <u>turnover</u> line, we should certainly be considering the increase at the <u>profit</u> line.

paid!

Another example:

Let's imagine the basic costs out of the £20,000 turnover on line 1 are in the order of £8,000. If we increase by 10% across the board (Number of customers, average value, average frequency), we create an additional turnover of £6,620.

Comparing this as an increase in the £12,000 profit (20,000-8000), we can see we have increased profits by 55%.

And all this increased by only 10% in the three key areas.

When we look at line 4, where we've increased the turnover by £11,680 and consider the increased profit, we can see we've increased profit by a massive 97%. And this is at only a 20% increase in customers, a 20% increase in average order value and a 10% increase in average order frequency.

I urge you to create a spreadsheet similar to the table I've shown you and play with different numbers (percentages), starting by adding accurate numbers from your own business.

- How many clients/customers do you currently have?
- What is your average order value?
- What is your average order frequency?
- What is your average retention rate?

If you'd like the complete lists of answers for the 4 questions, just pop over to:
www.thepaidbook.com/downloads

Retention Rates:

I remember a conversation with Professor John Murphy. He was the visiting professor of customer excellence at Manchester Business School, Manchester University. He explained that his research indicated that when customers stated they were 'Satisfied', they were 65% loyal. However, when they stated they were 'Very Satisfied', they were 95% loyal.

What an amazing uplift in loyalty (which, for our conversation, we'll call - retention) when customers/clients are happy to state that they are 'very satisfied'.

This prompts the question:

How can we increase our customer survey responses from 'Satisfied' to 'Very Satisfied'?

In your own business, you will know how much an increase in retention rate is likely to add to your bottom-line profit. I suggest you look back into your business records to see if any of your clients have quietly quit their relationship with you.

And if so, what would be the value of those clients in the period since they left?

Increasing the Retention Rate:

#1: Systemised Referral Process:

One of the most powerful ways to increase the retention rate, particularly in a consultancy business where the relationship is so important, is to have a 'Systemised Referral Process' in place.

The majority of consultants, coaches, trainers, speakers, accountants and small-business owners I speak to are convinced that referral business tends to convert at a higher percentage than cold leads. However, I'm not sure this is accurate. And I will cover this in greater detail in a moment.

I do believe it is essential (if we require an ongoing stream of qualified leads) to put in place a systemised referral process.

Here is why:

Asking our current happy clients, who are experiencing uplifts in their business because of our intervention, for referrals regularly has two major benefits.

"When the first leaf falls, we know that autumn has come to the world"

Benefit #1:

We find out, earlier than usual, if the client has a problem which means we might lose them. The above expression prompts us to ensure we are finding out when the first leaf falls.

You will probably spot a change in habit patterns as the first indication of a problem. A client, who normally returns your phone calls or emails almost immediately, suddenly starts to be tardy in their responses.

The client who asked for your opinion in the context of what you help them with; starts to take action without reference to you, and you only find out later.

A mutual connection mentions something the client has said that is surprising to you. Because usually, they will mention it to you first.

As it can be very expensive to gain a new client (subject to a lead generation strategy and costs), it makes sense to maintain our connections, continue to help them and continue to be paid.

Benefit #2:

Creating a stream of qualified referrals. What better than having a zero-cost lead generation system where our current happy clients continually refer their friends and colleagues to us.

However, it's important that we create a process, a system, a way of doing this so that it doesn't become simply (like most people's) ad hoc!

When would be the right time for you to ask for referrals?

Some of my clients feel the right time is once their clients have experienced their intervention and have reaped the rewards and benefits. Others have stated they'd be happy to ask at any time.

My personal preference is not 'time based' but 'feeling based'.

I feel it is appropriate to ask for referrals at any point when my client is 'happy'. They may be happy because we've met each other. They may be happy because I shared an idea with them in our first meeting, which they can see will be so powerful, simple to implement, and profitable. And they want their friends and connections to know about it too.

Obviously, it's your choice. Question: what will your strategy be?

Referral Conversion Rate:

I previously mentioned the idea that some people feel the conversion rate of referrals is higher than leads generated in other ways.

My personal feeling on this is: It totally depends on how we ask and what we ask the referrer to do for us.

If the referrer simply gives us a list of names and numbers to call (out of the blue), this may not be much better than a list from Yellow Pages.

If the referrer is happy for us to 'use their name' when we call their connections as an introduction, then this can improve the likelihood of a successful outcome.

But even better...

If the referrer is happy to call their connection, introduce us, explain why it would be a good idea for their connection to speak to us and perhaps even provide a testimonial - now we're talking!

The chances of this type of referral conversion are obviously much higher.

4 extra ideas for you on increasing your retention rate:

#2: Essential Long-Term Extras

Is there any part of your offering that could be termed an 'essential long-term extra'?

Here's an example.

I've seen a variety of offerings in the marketplace where consultancy and advice are being offered; however, as a bonus, a new 'software programme' is also included. Usually, it's included for 12 months. However, at the end of that 12 months, there is a monthly subscription to pay in the area of $50-$100.

Naturally, this is an excellent bonus and, as a retention strategy, very powerful. If the new software is essential to the running of the business in a new way, this makes it very difficult for the client to leave. Naturally, this must be an integrity-based offer.

#3: Ebbinghaus Effect

I've previously mentioned providing additional material to help your clients revisit the ideas you discussed and put them into practice. This is based on the Ebbinghaus Curve of Forgetting, which indicates that information needs to be revisited for it to become a long-term memory.

What additional informational product or service can you offer to help your clients?

- Could you perhaps record your meeting with them and provide the recording in an online portal for them to access.
- Can you create templates to make it easier for them to use your ideas?
- Could you offer additional coaching or additional services?

#4: WOW! Customer Service

There is a great deal of conversation these days about the level of customer service suppliers provide. However, we only have to look online to see the power of reviews in people's decision-making about who they will buy from.

We can consider three ways to interact with our clients and provide different levels of customer service.

We can 'HOW ' them:

This means we have provided a level of service which was 'How' they expected it to be. No better, no worse.

We can 'OOW ' them:

This means we have provided a lower service level than they expected.

Let me give you a couple of ideas from my experience. I remember turning up at a client's premises to find a change to the car parking arrangements. There were newly marked spaces outside the front door of the building for the directors' cars. The visitor spaces were at the far end of the building!

I can't imagine what they were thinking. Naturally, I pointed this out to them.

At a different client's office (they were involved in the metal business), I was delighted to see that a metal sign bearing my name had been screwed to the wall for my parking place right outside the front door.

paid!

Sadly, they had misspelt my name!

And that leads us to other ways to 'wow' our clients.

We forget their names. We forget their preferences. We forget details of other people in our lives whom they have previously discussed. We don't take the appropriate level of notes from our meeting and so have to start the next meeting catching up with things we really should know.

I'm sure you can think of many more that, like me, you may have been guilty of doing, or we've seen others commit these sins!

We can 'OOW' them:
Yes, we can provide a level of service that is so exceptional that our clients will be telling everyone about it. We follow up every meeting by sending them a personalised card in the mail with our thanks, even a small gift.

We start the very first meeting we have with the client by giving them a copy of our latest book. Talk about positioning!

We keep our promises. If a particular book is mentioned during the conversation that the client may not have read (I will check to ensure they haven't read it), then after the meeting, we can buy that book online and arrange to have it sent to them.

I remember, during the sale of my business some years ago, a mainboard director of the purchasing company came to my house and having met my wife, asked her for her birthday details. He made a great show of writing it down in his little notebook but nothing ever happened. That is the typical 'broken implied promise' action.

In what other ways can you 'WOW' your clients? I'm confident you can think of many more.

#5: Regular Contact

I'm somewhat surprised to hear from people they are concerned about emailing their clients and contacts too often.

If we have an email list of potential and current clients, separating the two will be very easy. With a prospect list, I believe we should contact them at least once a week. Not with an offer every single time. Not with something they need to click every single time. But with valuable information relevant to the reason why they signed up for our list.

A number of people seem to have a 'don't contact list' rather than a 'contact list '.

If people unsubscribe because we are contacting them with quality information, it is highly unlikely they will turn into long-term clients.

paid!

Increasing the Number of Customers:

Here are three extra ideas you can use to increase the number of customers or clients:

Introductory Events:

I must admit I love holding seminars and webinars. Because it enables me to share several of my tried and tested, and proven ideas with potential clients, it becomes a showcase. So, rather than asking them to 'trust me', I'm actually demonstrating my ideas work and can produce the results they are looking for.

A typical one-hour free webinar advertised on social media is the perfect opportunity to show potential clients what we can do and make a powerful offer for them to buy an initial product at a low entry price or even take a survey to tell us what help they require.

I found this works well with a three-hour seminar or even a whole-day event. With whole-day events, I usually run mine from 9:30 am to 4:30 pm. On the whole-day event, I will make my offering during the mid-afternoon coffee break.

Sometimes, I make the offering just before the lunch break. This timing can obviously be tested with your marketplace.

The Four Questions of Business Growth

Lead Generation Using a Free Book/Free Report:

Over many years I've experienced great success in lead generation by offering a free report or a free copy of one of my books. This works so well because by changing the title of the book or report to focus on the pain a potential client is experiencing or the gain they wish to achieve, we can separate our marketing from other people.

One of my most successful campaigns, which ran for many years, offered a free report with the following lengthy title:

"The Shocking Report: The 7 BIG mistakes business owners are unwittingly making costing them a fortune in lost turnover, lost profits, and what's even worse lost personal cash - and how to avoid them!"

This 33-word title would seem to be a mistake. However, it's probably the highest-pulling lead generation report

I've ever created. Why? Because it clearly states who it's for, what their problem might be, and the fact a solution is available.

And this is a very simple formula to use for creating titles:

- Person
- Problem
- Possible solution

When we use this formula, we only attract those who resonate with the title. Yes, we can use a very short title. For example: "Back Pain?".

Whenever you're crafting the title of your book, report, seminar or webinar, I suggest you consider the idea that we want our reader to think, "This is for me" rather than thinking, "Is it for me?" You can imagine how much more engaged they will be with the first thought.

Using a physical book sent in the post is also a very powerful lead generation strategy - and one I've often used. We position ourselves as an authority figure and provide a valuable product free of charge. What better way could there be to engage a client who is looking for the solution we have.

Endorsed Marketing

I was fortunate to get to know the well-known marketer Jay Abraham. I attended his three-day marketing seminar in Los Angeles and then hosted six of his 3-day seminars in the United Kingdom.

The Four Questions of Business Growth

During one of our conversations, I asked him, "Jay, if you had to get rid of all your marketing ideas except one, which one would you keep?" His immediate reply was, "Endorsed promotions".

By this, he meant if he could get a list owner, who had a relationship with the people on their list, to endorse the offering and offer made by Jay, then the strong likelihood was the conversion rates would be extremely good.

I've used this idea. It has worked very well for me. For example, I approached a well-known fitness person in the UK and asked them to endorse one of my audio programmes to their franchisees. The programme was called, "Accomplishment The Science and Practice" and detailed numerous ideas on personal development and success.

Having listened to the free copy of the programme I gave them, they were happy to endorse it, and the direct mailing pulled over a 50% conversion rate. The power of endorsement!

Question:
Who do you know who knows the people you want to know? And could you, by explaining the benefits you can bring to those people, ask them to endorse your product or service?

paid!

Increasing the Average Order Value:

Testing prices:

I've covered a number of ideas for you throughout this book on increasing prices. But the truth is, no one knows what someone else will pay, and the only way to find out is to test it.

Sometimes, a higher price will produce an increase in order value. Sometimes a lower price will increase the number of clients or customers who engage with us, and therefore turnover goes up because of that increase.

Of course, we need to test prices regularly to see at which price our current and potential clients are most responsive.

For many years I've been dismayed at the lower levels of fees many consultants and similar professionals charge their clients. And invariably, when I suggest their fees are increased, I receive reports saying how easy it was to increase turnover profits and income.

Payments Terms:

Many tests have shown that just having the right payment terms can increase the average order value (and increase the number of new clients we attract).

For example:

If you are running a seminar, then offering two or three payments rather than one payment has been shown to increase how many people will sign up and show up.

When I was running my 1/3/12 process of a one-day seminar into a three-day weekend into a 12-month mentoring programme, I decided to test offering a three-part payment offer. Of course, with a three-month payment programme, you get the money all paid within two months.

This increased sales by over 30%. And not only that, but it increased sales of the offer made at the three-day event, namely, the 12 monthly mentoring programme.

How many payments are in the payment plan?

Some years ago, I heard about a well-known American presenter, author and experienced marketer who carried out a 3-way test.

He offered a product with a payment of $200 and made a few sales. He then offered the same product but with two payments of $100, doubling the sales. He then did the third test and offered the product but with three payments of $100 (A 50% increase in price) and added 50% to the already doubled sales figures.

Until we test, we simply do not know the price and the payment terms most acceptable to our audience.

Deluxe:

Of course, no conversation about an increase in the average order value could ever pass by without mentioning having a deluxe and double deluxe version.

Again, let me urge you to spend the time going back through the ideas I've previously shared about creating your deluxe versions and then testing those versions in the marketplace.

If, like me, you manage to secure a 10%/20% deluxe take-up, what might that do to your 'average' order values?

I found that once I know the likely financial impact of these ideas, I'm prompted to take action.

Always on the basis that:

> *"Money is the silent applause for*
> *a job well done and*
> *value delivered to others"*
>
> Peter Thomson

Increasing the Average Order Frequency:

Now let's look at 3 ideas which can help us increase the average order frequency.

Don't sell one-off interventions:

Sadly, I see so many coaches, consultants, and other professionals only ever offering one-off sessions and then having to 'sell' subsequent sessions during those sessions.

Far better to make an arrangement with the client for a six-month contract with a breakpoint at three months where results can be reviewed, and confirmation of the next three months agreed upon.

This works well for clients because they know we are committed to them for a specified period of time, and it works well for us because we know what our potential income will be from the client over that period.

You and I are fully aware that most of our work has a cumulative effect as we share more ideas and the client implements the ideas to gain increasing results.

A one-off session is often called a 'warm bath' or 'whitewash' experience, where the client gets very warm whilst we are there and cold again as soon as we leave. Or, we cover the client in a whitewash during our time with them, but it soon washes off as they experience life and their usual daily challenges.

Those types of sessions benefit nobody. The client isn't committed for the necessary period of time, and when they do not get the results they were hoping for, our reputation suffers as well.

It's much better to arrange for an appropriate number of months of interventions.

paid!

Rolling contract:

Another way to increase the average order frequency is to engage in a rolling contract with the client with a determined notice period.

For example:

We might start with a three-month arrangement with a review period and then move on to a rolling three-month contract with a three-month notice period.

Or, perhaps a six-month arrangement followed by a one-month rolling contract. And many other variations.

Just imagine how this creates far higher numbers when you are examining your average order frequency.

A monthly subscription programme:

I've previously mentioned the Ebbinghaus Effect. To counteract this and help the client get even greater long-term benefits from the help we give them, we could offer an ongoing subscription programme or additional coaching service.

I've often asked consultants and trainers how many people they help over the course of a year. Not just the direct client but the people working for the client's business. Often this can be 1000 people. I then suggested a follow-up programme, delivered monthly at a nominal figure of, say, £10 per person per month.

Not only are we providing greater value, but we could generate an additional income of £120,000 per annum.

This works! It benefits everyone concerned.

Plus, it brings us to the idea of taking our knowledge, experience and expertise (plus our take) and turning them into a variety of different informational products.

What might you be able to do to help your clients on a monthly basis following the work you've done with them.

Subscription And Mentoring Programmes:

In addition to having a follow-up subscription or coaching programme, you could have a standalone subscription and/or mentoring programme.

A monthly webinar where members attend for a couple of hours a month, during which time you share with them your knowledge and experience and help them get the outcomes they are looking for and solve the problems that arise in their businesses.

Let's say the subscription was £100 per month, and you had just 50 members. That's an annual income of £60,000; after marketing costs, the 'run on cost' is very low.

A monthly mentoring group where you meet with the members for a one-day session every month. If you had 10 members paying £500 a month, that too would be an annual income of £60,000.

What variations of this would work for you and the type of client you work with?

And how much extra income could this generate for you?

So, there we have it – The four golden questions of business growth.

Now you are aware of them and some of the answers I would urge you to take these three actions:

1. Continually ask yourself these questions and develop more relevant answers for you and your business.
2. Be aware – when you are dealing with other businesses (even as simple as buying a burger) where the supplier is obviously working on increasing the number of customers, increasing the average order value, increase in the average order frequency or increasing the retention rate. How many times have we been asked, "Would you like fries with that?"
3. Go to this address:
   www.thepaidbook.com/downloads
   and get the full list of answers to the four golden questions.

REFRESHER 7

1. Four Questions Of Business Growth.

2. When the first leaf falls, we know that autumn has come to the world.

3. A Systemised Referral Process.

4. Offsetting the Ebbinghaus Effect by providing follow-up material.

5. Wow! Customer service. Wow! How! Oow!

6. Maintaining regular contact.

7. Offering an "Away-motivated titled" report to attract your "love to deal with" clients.

8. Endorsed Marketing. When the list owner, with a relationship with the people on their list, endorses your offering; you are likely to have high conversion rates.

9. Don't sell one off interventions. Offer rolling contracts.

In the next chapter, we will look at why it is essential you become an author and have the opportunity to use your 'writings' for positioning, persuasion and profit.

paid!

Action Plan

Actions	Priority	When by	Done

Chapter Eight

Why You MUST Write a Book

Of all the ways of differentiating ourselves from the vast crowd of other coaches and consultants, there is one that stands head and shoulders above the rest.

You must be an author!

Now, this can be as simple as creating a short report, a tips booklet or even a white paper. Whatever it is, we need 'something' with our name as the author (and, of course, the strapline) on it, which we can use in a number of different ways.

There's a common expression in marketing consultancy services which is known as 'A Category of One '. This means if we are able to create this category, this is yet another way of separating ourselves from the others in the marketplace.

paid!

For example:

If you only deal with a certain type of business, in a certain area, in a certain market, offering a very specific service, then you are able to clearly state that you are the leading (or one of the leading) authorities in that area.

If your offering is so generalised, you are one of the thousands, if not millions, then how is a potential client able to pick you rather than others?

As a colleague of mine often states, we need to become our client's natural, emotional and logical choice.

When to write your book:

When we look at sports stars, we find they write their book (or perhaps have it ghost-written) whilst they are at the height of their fame and popularity. This, of course, maximises sales.

When we look at successful business leaders, they write their books when they have reached a high level of success and recognition. This maximises sales.

When we look at politicians, they write their book once they have left politics, but whilst they are still well-known personalities with a large following. This maximises sales.

For people like you and me, however, we need to create our 'book' as soon as we start being a coach or consultant (or even a trainer, a speaker, an accountant, or a small business owner).

Why? Because we need to use that book to position ourselves in the marketplace, gain credibility and recognition and have an opportunity to share our knowledge, experience, and expertise.

When you stand on your book, you are more visible to the marketplace.

The 15 Reasons to Write Your Book

Here are 15 reasons why I believe it is essential to become an author.

1. Establishing Our Authority:

Writing a business book establishes our authority in our chosen field immediately. I mentioned before how wonderful it is to attend a meeting with a new client and pass over our book, so we start by creating a feeling of reciprocation or obligation. (In an integrity-based way). If we feel bold enough, we can even gently ask the potential client, "Would you like me to sign it for you?"

In his brilliant books on persuasion, Professor Robert Cialdini talks about the power of authority and explains there are 3 factors.

1. Title
2. Trappings
3. Clothing

paid!

A book with our name as the author fits perfectly into factors #1 and #2.

2. Differentiating ourselves from the competition:

How many other coaches and consultants do you think have already created their business book? I know the answer to this question. Very few! As soon as we become authors, we widen the separation gap and give our clients yet another reason to consider us their first choice. We can showcase our unique expertise throughout the pages of our latest book.

Yes, why stop with one book?

In a moment, I'll show you how you can get complete instructions on creating your book. Once you know how, I'm confident you'll want to become a regular writer.

3. Your Personal Brand:

When we looked at the factors of your personal brand after completing the 'tray' exercise, we realised how important it is to have a brand that matches who we are and how we help our clients.

What better way to establish ourselves as an authority, as different, separate from the market than by being an author, especially a prolific author.

4. The Ideal Lead Generator:

In the next chapter, I'll go into detail about how you use your business book as the ideal lead magnet/generator and, by doing so, how you are able to reach those potential clients not found on the usual lists.

5. Wider Audience:

When we have a book available for sale in different places (on our website, via links from our social media pages, bookstores, airports, almost anywhere), we send out a team of silent salespeople who can attract new connections and new clients for us.

My first book, 'Sell Your Way to The Top' was for sale at Schiphol airport in Amsterdam. A fellow consultant spotted it, was intrigued by the title and bought a copy. After that, he contacted me and arranged for me to speak three times for one of his European clients.

It just goes to show how many wide-ranging connections can be made by having a book to offer.

6. Establishing Thought Leadership:

The more content we put into our marketplace (provided the content is first-rate), the sooner we are recognised as a Thought Leader in our chosen field.

- Is there a particular marketplace you would like to dominate?
- Is there a particular reputation you would like to have?
- Is there a particular sector of clients you'd like to work with?

If the answer is "Yes" to these questions, then the way to expand our reach and increase the awareness of the market of the power of our ideas can be achieved by writing a high-quality content book.

7. Passive income:

The expression 'passive income' is often discussed, and few opportunities exist to create a truly passive income. Certainly, with a book, if it's for sale on our website or the various other areas I mentioned previously, then sales can take place without any further activity on our part. This is passive income.

However, to produce further income, it will take some thought, some preparation, and some action. Later in this chapter, I'll explain a number of ways in which you can repurpose the ideas of your book into many other informational products.

And by doing so, you can create multiple streams of income.

8. Developing New Skills:

Many of my clients, who have written their own books following my ideas and methods, have reported to me the skills they developed in the process; they've been able to take into other areas of their business and their life.

Trainers often report that they now use my process to write a book to create their training courses.

The simple book-writing system I've developed can be used to create so many different information-sharing products.

9. Increasing Knowledge via Content Research:

During the course of writing your book, you'll no doubt be doing research. Even if it's simply looking for appropriate quotes to scatter through the manuscript.

I've found as I'm writing new products, notes for webinars, mentoring programmes and client meetings - the ideas I find online, in books, by attending other webinars, and even on YouTube - all add to my knowledge base.

"It's what we learn today,
that gives value
to what we learnt yesterday"
Zig Ziglar

As lifelong learners, you and I continually increase our knowledge and weaving the new ideas into what we already know continues to create new thoughts, new ideas and messages to help our clients gain the successes they desire.

10. Creating a Media Presence:

Over my years in business, I've been lucky to engage with the media in a positive way through radio, TV, shopping channels, online and newspapers.

I know many of those connections were made because I am an author.

If you want to increase your media presence, once you have your book, you can engage in some PR activity, sending copies to those radio and TV stations and newspapers you wish to connect with. I've seen clients become the 'go to person' for specific topic areas in local and national media.

Do you want to create a media presence?

11. Creating Opportunities:

Once you have your book (or books) and the other informational products that will spring from them – then you have an ideal team of silent salespeople (as I previously mentioned) who can gain connections for you for speaking engagements, workshops, consulting projects or any of the many other services you may offer.

I suggest you make a list of the people you want to send a free copy of the book to, so you can build even more of the ideal connections you want.

Here is the process:

Phone call/book/ phone call.

It's better if it isn't you who makes the first phone call. Perhaps have a colleague who can do that, or if not, you can engage an outside company to do it.

The call is made to the assistant of the person you wish to send your book to, asking this question, "(Your name) would like to send a free copy of their new book (Title of the book) to (Name), is it better I send it to you or directly to (Name)?

Once the book has been sent, a follow-up call is made to the assistant, mentioning the book, checking it has arrived safely and asking for an appointment with the potential client.

This 'phone call/book/phone call system can work extremely well. You realise a degree of reciprocation/obligation has been created by sending the free book.

Fortunately, this is not a very expensive route to market, as you can target just a few potential clients at a time.

I recall a member of one of my groups sent out her tips booklets with a cover letter to a number of potential clients. One client liked the booklet so much that they ordered 2,000 copies at £5 per copy.

I'll explain more about using your book as a lead generator.

12. Building Online Visibility and the Following:

In an ever-increasing online marketplace, we can build online visibility and a following by providing good quality content targeted to our intended audience. What better way than the ideas you've already put into your book repurposed for short sharp content in a variety of different formats.

Asking questions of those initial followers can give you further insight into ideas you can expand on for future content.

13. Making a Difference:

I'm certain you and I are very focused on making a positive difference in the world. After all, that's what we do when we are helping our clients.

Part of the challenge is how we impact the maximum number of people. So naturally, having a book and offering it through all the usual marketing channels is the ideal way to expand our reach and help others.

A number of my clients have gone down the road of setting up a foundation where the aim is to help those who are financially unable to access all their ideas and help them to be more successful in life.

14. Leaving a Legacy:

A successful businessman friend once told me, "When I die, I don't want to leave a dirty smudge but a big X to mark where I was!" I think we can understand what he means.

What a perfect way of leaving a legacy of all the knowledge, experience, expertise, and our 'take 'on everything we learned; so, the current and future generations can benefit from it all.

I've always considered how amazing (and cost-effective) it is to buy a book and learn all the life lessons the author has gathered - and has taken the time to share.

When I look at my 'body of work 'and see all the books, audios, videos, tips booklets and so on; I am pleased and proud I took the time to cascade my thoughts onto paper/audio/video.

> *"The mass of men lead lives of quiet desperation, and go to the grave with the song still in them"*
>
> Henry David Thoreau
> in his classic book 'Walden'

A book is an ideal way to share your 'song'.

15. The best business card:

And, as I've touched on a number of times throughout this book, what better business card could we ever have than a copy of our own book.

Being able to offer our book (in physical or download form) is just wonderful. It separates us from the crowd and immediately establishes our credibility and authority.

Bonus Idea: Creating a business and a life of choice

Taking our knowledge, experience and expertise and cascading it into a booklet, a book and then a variety of different informational products helps us create a business and life of choice for ourselves.

When we invest the time to write, create and market our ideas in different ways we are being paid interest on those efforts.

> *"Chop Your Own Wood and it Will Warm You Twice"*
>
> Henry Ford

And what wonderful choices we have:

1. We get to choose why we do what we do (our purpose)
2. We get to choose who we work with

3. We get to choose when we work - dates, times, months, years

4. We get to choose where we work. The beauty of sharing your knowledge is it can often be done from almost anywhere we have an Internet connection and an appropriate device. We can be sitting on a beach, on the hillside overlooking a lake or anywhere that takes our fancy.

5. We get to choose how much we are paid

6. And we get to choose how we do what we do.

Isn't this the way to live our lives?

A life of choice, a life of freedom, a life of making a positive difference in the world.

There is an addition to this. And it's summed up in the following expression, which I wrote some years ago:

In the beginning you do a lot of work
You don't get paid for,
So in the future if you get paid
For a lot of work
You no long have to do

Peter Thomson

Repurposing Your Knowledge:

Here are 20 ways to take the knowledge and experience, and expertise you have cascaded into your book and repurpose them to create numerous ways to help your clients.

1. Streaming video/audio
2. PDF
3. Tips Booklet
4. Book – softback/ hardback
5. 4-Ring binder
6. Training/ In house seminar
7. Coaching (individuals/ group) (online/offline)
8. Mentoring (individuals/ group)
9. (online/offline)
10. Webinar
11. Seminar
12. Bootcamp / Retreat
13. Teleseminar
14. Podcast
15. TV appearance/Online TV
16. Continuity (newsletter/ audio/video/print/ download)
17. Anthology book with other authors
18. Application (mobile phone)
19. Report/Guide/White Paper/Review
20. Licence your material

If you'd like a free copy of my complete list of "The 79 Ways to Repurpose Your Content", then go to: www.thepaidbook. com/downloads

Writing Your Own Book:

If you feel it would be a great idea to write your own business book, so you can use it as the ideal business card, and a powerful lead magnet, I will be delighted to help you.

One of my books is called:

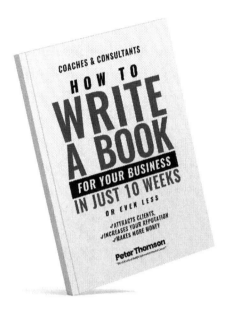

Your Free Copy:

Based on what I've been saying about the power of using your book to engage potential clients, I'm certain you're not surprised I'd like to give you a free copy. So, if you'd like to immediately access a pdf version and get started on writing your book, then go to:

https://www.thepaidbook.com/downloads

REFRESHER 8

1. Why You Must be an Author..

2. 15 reasons to write your book.
    1. Establish your authority
    2. Differentiate yourself from the competition
    3. Build your personal brand
    4. The ideal lead generator
    5. Reach a wider audience
    6. Establish thought leadership
    7. Generate passive income
    8. Develop new skills
    9. Increase knowledge via content research
    10. Create a media presence
    11. Create opportunities
    12. Build online visibility and a following
    13. Make a positive difference in the world
    14. Leave a lasting legacy
    15. The best business card you ever had

3. Creating a business and a life of choice

4. Repurposing your knowledge into a vast array of different informational products.

paid!

Action Plan

Actions	Priority	When by	Done

CHAPTER NINE

Creating Your Lead Magnet

By now, you know I am really keen on you having a business book with your name as the author.

And the major reason for this is – you will be able to use it as the most powerful lead-generation magnet you could ever have.

And by so doing, attract only those clients you love to help. Those who have a problem you know you can solve or those who have an opportunity which you can help them capitalise upon.

In Michael Basch's words, these people will 'stay, say, and pay'. Their retention rate is high. They regularly and willingly provide testimonials and references. And they happily pay your fees on time.

paid!

Previously we talked about having a systemised referral process and using your book as the introduction to the referrals you have received from your current happy clients. This is, again, using your powerful lead generation magnet. Your book!

The Challenge:

The challenge we face in our marketing activities is other people in our industry who provide similar services are out there - marketing to all the usual lists, the usual places in social media and even pay-per-click adverts targeting the same people we wish to talk to.

The Solution:

The solution is to find a way of attracting those ideal clients who are not necessarily appearing in 'all the usual places'.

Here is how we do it:

We use a book if it has the right title. Or we create a lead magnet report with a title to attract the people we wish to speak to.

Educational Marketing:

It is much better to provide high-quality, usable, valuable information to our clients through a book, report, checklist, quiz, a webinar - rather than simply 'asking them to buy' right at the start of our relationship.

When we engage in 'content marketing' that has value in and of itself as part of our lead generation activities, we are far more likely to build rapport faster and attract those ideal clients.

Outer And Inner Labels:

You <u>can't</u> find people who 'fear selling' on a list - unless they've bought before and then through 'Voice of Customer' research.

You <u>can</u> find people who own snakes - they'll be on a list somewhere - you <u>can't</u> find people on a list who want to buy snakes.

However, you <u>can</u> reach out to people who 'fear selling' or 'are thinking of buying a snake' with your book or your lead generation report.

The people found in the usual places (and there is no reason why we may not do this as well as our other marketing strategies) are identified by a number of factors.

If you are a member of LinkedIn and use their sales navigator programme, then you will easily find a list of the approximately 27 criteria you can select when searching for connections. This is an excellent list of what I call "outer labels".

paid!

Examples of Outer Labels:

- Title
- Profession
- Position
- Location
- Company Size
- Previous purchases

Examples of Inner Labels:

Let's start by considering some examples of 'Inner Labels':

Intentions
Feelings
Hopes/desires/dreams
Pains/problems
Goals

If we create a report or write a book where the title clearly talks to intended clients' intentions, feelings, hopes, desires, dreams, pains, problems, goals or a variety of other <u>inner</u> thoughts, then they are far more likely to respond to our marketing message.

And not only that, but they also respond positively and immediately, willing to give us their details.

Creating Your Lead Magnet

Insider Secret:

On the landing page for our free report/book, it is usual to ask for somebody's name, email address and perhaps even more information about them. It's commonly agreed the more information you ask for, the lower will be your 'sign up rate'.

I found, however, (by testing) I could increase the <u>level of qualification</u> of the potential client who was signing up for my free report/book by asking for a specific piece of information.

Yes, I included a field asking for their phone number. Many people suggested I was crazy and would dramatically diminish the signup rate.

First, it did not diminish the signup rate dramatically; there was a slight fall. However (and this is such an important point), the <u>quality</u> of the leads increased, as did our conversion rate.

Why did this happen?

Simply because I was asking my website visitors to the landing page to act in a way that confirmed their trust in me. Who do we gladly give our phone number to? Only people we trust!

And by asking visitors for their phone numbers, I was asking them to treat me like they treat other people they trust.

And, of course, having the phone number made it far easier for us to follow up with the person who had signed up for

paid!

the book or report. Not only using a series of emails but with a telephone call to book an appointment.

A Real-World Example:

As I mentioned previously, over 25 years ago, I created a report called:

The Shocking Report:
"The 7 BIG mistakes business owners are unwittingly making costing them a fortune in lost turnover, lost profits, and what's even worse lost personal cash - and how to avoid them!"

This formed the central part of my marketing activities for several years and was instrumental in bringing thousands of leads to the top of my marketing funnel.

You can clearly see the title and subtitle of the report are targeting the three key factors we discussed before:

1. The person - business owner
2. The problem - making the 7 big mistakes and the downsides of that: lost turnover, lost profits, lost personal cash
3. And a possible solution - how do you avoid the 7 big mistakes?

This is a perfect 'inner label' title.

My questions to you are:

Creating Your Lead Magnet

1. What is the biggest problem or pain your client is suffering (In the context of what you do)?
2. What are the downsides of the problem?
3. What are the possible opportunities they have?
4. What are the upsides of capitalising on those opportunities?
5. How can you clearly state that problem and its downsides so it will be attractive to your prospective client in a book title or report title?

Here are some examples:

My Facebook advertising has stopped working!

Back pain?

Where do I find more salespeople?

How to gain a stream of qualified leads without breaking the bank

I know you have the idea and will be able to craft different titles for your books and reports so you can test them in your marketplace.

Away And Towards Titles:

When crafting the title, it's worthwhile to consider testing 'away motivated' against 'towards motivated' titles.

For example:

Away motivated: The 7 big mistakes business owners are unwittingly making... and how to avoid them.

Towards motivated: The 7 (little known) secrets of increasing turnover, profits and personal cash...

Whilst I've found 'away motivated' titles tend to produce high conversion rates with a 'cold audience', I'm always testing to discover different ways to increase the conversion rates.

Landing Pages:

If your marketing messages contain sufficient information for prospective clients to decide, they want to sign up for the book or report. I suggest not making them take time to read the same information on the landing page.

Over my marketing career, I've carried out many tests. One of these was to remove the sales page and take responders directly to a simple signup page for the free report. This removal increased signup rates by 100%. Yes, it doubled the signup rate.

An Unusual Communication Method:

When using a telephone call to follow up with someone who has downloaded/received your book or report, it's essential to consider the questions you or one of your colleagues is going to ask.

Having tested a variety of questions, here is a surprising insight.

Creating Your Lead Magnet

When I've asked seminar audience members what questions they believe we should ask someone who has downloaded our book/report, these are the type of questions they've suggested:

1. What was the best part of the book?
2. What have you done with the ideas?
3. Have you read it?
4. What surprised you?
5. What did you already know?
6. What have you decided to action?

These and similarly phrased questions <u>must be avoided</u> at all costs!

Let's examine what's going on in the potential client's mind (once they have received/downloaded the report/book) and what actions they are likely to have taken:

Like many people and me, I'm sure you download numerous reports and information from the Internet. However, you probably haven't read all of them. In fact, I found a majority of people who download information <u>do not read</u> it or at least do not read all of it.

So, if we ask any of the questions I've just mentioned (or similarly phrased questions), we will <u>not</u> get a positive response.

And when this happens (we get a negative response), the potential client will not wish to go to the next stage in a sales and marketing process until, in their own words, "I've read the book!"

Here is a far better series of questions:

1. Is that your 'first name'? The client will say, "Yes".
2. You requested a copy of the "Name of book or report, yes?"
   The client will respond with, "Yes".
3. The Magic Question:

   "I don't suppose you've had chance to read it yet, have you?"

The answer most often given is, "Oh, no I haven't got round to it yet."

And you can see how easy it is to engage in conversation about people being busy and how much else there is to do in life.

We are focusing question #3 on the fact that most people will <u>not</u> have read it, and therefore why on earth would we ask them if they have; or ask for details of what they've learnt from the report/book!

It's far better to focus the question...

On what is likely to have happened.

In a few cases, where the client will have you read the report or book and respond with, "Oh, actually I have read it", we (or our colleague making the call) will simply continue with the conversation.

"Excellent, (and into the rest of the appointment-making call)

The script I developed, which my colleagues use, continues in this way:

"Well, the reason why Peter wanted you to have a copy of his latest book was to introduce you to the idea of XXX. He's launching his new product/service called ABC. Is this something you might be interested in knowing details about?"

You'll note my use of the word 'might' as I'm a great believer in a soft approach.

The call continues, and an appointment is made.

This approach and script have proven to be so successful in gaining well-qualified leads.

I heartily recommend you try it for yourself.

The Big Book Mistake:

One of those mistakes I see regularly made by new authors is using their book to fulfil too many roles. They use it as a giveaway, they use it as a money maker, and they use it as a book. And yes, a book can do all of these things.

However, I believe it's far better, because of the importance of the title of the book/report, to consider either:

1. Writing a series of short books
2. Using the same book but changing the title so it's appropriate for a lead generator when we target your potential clients' inner labels.

There is no reason, as it's our book, why we cannot change the title of the book without changing anything on the inside.

As 'print on demand' is so widely available, we can produce one book at a time, or 50 or 1,000 - the choice is ours. Though I would urge you to avoid printing large amounts.

I saw a client who'd been on a 'book writing retreat' following erroneous advice and had printed 1,000 copies of his book. When I spoke to him later, he still had 900 copies in his garage.

The book's title as a lead generator may not be the best title for other uses. For example, the book's strapline sometimes makes it a better 'normal' title, whereas the more powerful, engaging title is better for lead generation.

How Many Pages?

How many pages does your book need to be classed as a book?

Is it 100, is it 200, is it 20? No one really knows the real answer to this question because it is an opinion.

In the same vein, when does a report become a book?

The good news - we get to decide.

There has been a growth recently in short books. Books in the range between 60 - 80 pages. This has been led by the highly successful Dan Sullivan (https://www.strategiccoach.

com/) and his series of short books. When I interviewed Dan, he told me he had targeted to write 4 books a year for 25 years, a total of 100 books.

These books are jam-packed with tried and tested ideas and certainly don't need hundreds of pages to explain how we can benefit by using the powerful messages Dan details.

Why would we 'pad out' our book with unnecessary information for readers to plough through to get to the golden nuggets?

Other Lead Generation Ideas:

Here are some ideas for you to consider when offering your book as your lead generation magnet.

1. You could offer the book <u>completely free of charge</u>, with no fee for postage, packing or shipping and handling. Yes, there is a cost involved in this. However, it's fairly low, and even if it took 50 free books to secure 10 appointments to gain one client, then as a client acquisition cost in the area of £200, it would still, no doubt, be worthwhile.

I would certainly be very happy paying £200 to gain a new client.

2. You could offer the book as a PDF download. The slight challenge with this is that so many people download so many different PDFs from so many websites; they will likely not read many of them.

And if the initial information about the author isn't read by the person downloading - then a lot of the impact of 'being an author' is lost.

Nevertheless, it can work.

3. You could offer the first three chapters as a download PDF.

All of these offerings require a systemised follow-up process either by a series of emails or phone calls.

Being an author separates us from the crowd, gives us an ideal lead generation product, establishes our credibility, and gives us a base of information which we can turn into many different information products and services.

I cannot emphasise how important it is - to become an author.

In the next chapter, chapter 10, we look at "bringing it all together".

I'll give you my thoughts on how to create focus and in particular how to use the extremely simple yet powerful WWHAM process.

This is the process are use for all of my goals, because it gives me clarity and keeps me on track.

We'll look at the "Yesterday's Road Method" and I'll share the story of how it made me £1 million.

Creating Your Lead Magnet

With the Measurement Mistake, I'll explain how to avoid a commonly made error and we'll discover why, "Time and distance travelled compound is the effect of error".

REFRESHER 9

1. Creating Your Lead Magnet.

2. Outer and Inner Labels.

3. Reaching those people not found on the usual lists.

4. Attracting people by the title of your book or report focusing on their hopes, desires, fears and problems.

5. The Inside Secret. Asking for more details on the landing page in order to indicate a level of trust.

6. Away and towards motivated titles.

7. The Follow-Up Script. "I don't suppose you've had chance to read it yet have you?"

8. The Big Book Mistake. Trying to get one book to fulfil various functions.

9. Lead Generation Ideas. Offer the book completely free of charge. Offer the book as a PDF download. Offer the first three chapters free of charge.

Action Plan

Actions	Priority	When by	Done

CHAPTER TEN

Bringing It All Together

As you start out on the next chapter of your business, it would make sense to see how all of the elements we discussed throughout this book can come together to enable you to be rightfully rewarded for the significant positive differences you bring to your clients' lives.

Here are a variety of ideas you can use. I have tried and tested all of them in the real world.

Creating Focus:

I strongly suggest that you set goals before <u>every</u> client meeting, whether that's the first engagement or any subsequent intervention.

The way I do this is to be outwardly focused on all the benefits I can bring to my client - and nothing whatsoever about the benefits I receive. My benefits will be in my goal-setting pages for my business and my life.

Having set the goals for my client meetings, I will sign them and date them and re-visit them just before I meet with the client. This creates laser focus in my mind to help the client.

Some years ago, my then bank manager shared an idea with me that was so simple yet powerful at giving me clarity.

I read this wonderful quote in the book Decisive by Chip and Dan Heath:

"Resistance is created through a lack of clarity!"

And isn't this so true? The 4-stage process David Store (the bank manager) shared with me was: goal, plan, action, and feedback.

Over many years of using it, I altered it slightly, added a fifth stage and renamed it.

Now it's called:
WWHAM. Standing for: why, what, how, action, measure.

Bringing It All Together

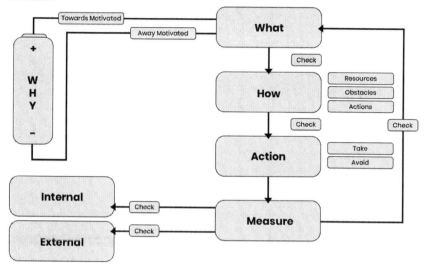

The WHY?

We start at the left-hand side of the diagram, looking at why we want to achieve whatever we want. And to build up the power in the why battery, we consider our 'away-motivation,' namely, what we <u>don't</u> want or are trying to move <u>away</u> from.

Then we consider our 'towards-motivation', knowing what we wish to <u>gain</u> or move <u>towards</u>.

I firmly believe we need clarity on both 'away and towards motivations', as clarity on these helps us achieve the outcomes we want.

> ## *"Away motivation is the catalyst for action, towards motivation is the continuation of action"*
> Peter Thomson

If we only ever use away motivation, then we will find ourselves in the wrongly named 'Comfort Zone'. It certainly isn't the comfort zone if we are continually not wanting to be poor but not wanting to be too rich. Not wanting to be too unhealthy and not wanting to be too fit.

Sadly, so many people live their lives in this zone without ever realising that's so much more as possible.

The What?

> ## *"If you don't know where you're going, all the roads lead there"*

Next, we go to the top of the right-hand side and look at what we want to achieve. Again, as I'm certain you already know, this must have sufficient detail for us to be able to audit the actions we subsequently take once we have clarity about what we're going to do to achieve what we say we want.

So, details such as numbers, dates, and times must all be included in the what, so we have complete clarity on the target we aim at.

The How:

"A goal without a plan is just a wish"

Antoine de Saint-Exupery

Now let's look at the how-to section, where you create the plan to achieve the goal. In a moment, I'll explain the 'Yesterday's Road Method', a proven way of knowing what you need to do to achieve any goal.

My suggestion is you start with a focused question:

"What do I possibly need to do to achieve this goal?" And simply write down whatever your mind tells you. After all, it knows you better than anybody else.

The beauty of this question is it is positioned past the point of having decided to achieve the goal. Otherwise, it would be phrased as, "Do I want to achieve this goal?".

And as our minds are brilliant at finding answers to focused questions, we can be certain they will provide the necessary answers.

The how also wants to consider:

1. What resources you will need to be able to achieve the goal. For example: Who can help you? And what do you need/want they to do. Money? Time?

2. Obstacles - what might get in your way. I love obstacles because by realising there is an obstacles I immediately know what I need to do to get round/over/through/under it.

And I'm certain you are well aware of the expression, "In every difficulty lies opportunity". So it is with obstacles. Perhaps we could considered, "In every obstacle lies the answer for its clearance".

"Organising Power is Inherent in Knowledge",
Deepak Chopra

3. Actions - what actions need to be taken by you or other to achieve the goal. These need to be consider in the how stage

The Actions:

Once we are clear on how we are going to achieve the goal, we now need to create an action plan, in prioritised order, with dates and checklists to ensure we stay on track.

Ideas you have captured in the how section will now need to turn into an action list.

The Yesterday's Road Method:

*"Ask yourself the easy questions
and you'll have a hard life.
Ask yourself the hard questions and
you'll have an easy life"*

Peter Thomson

This is an idea I developed over 30 years ago during the earn-out period when I sold my leasing business to a mainboard Stock Exchange London-based business. It works for any goal and lets us know the precise actions we need to take to achieve them.

This is what happened:

Having agreed on the sale for a lump sum in cash and a certain quantity of the buying company's shares, I would then receive a further tranche of shares if we hit the agreed-upon turnover targets.

Halfway through the earn-out year, we lost a major client. But we had done everything correctly. They simply moved out of the leasing space. This created a problem for me; it didn't look like we would hit the targeted turnover figures and, therefore, wouldn't get the second tranche of the earn-out payment.

I spent a great deal of time thinking about how to solve this problem and came up with The Yesterday's Road Method.

paid!

Using it, we soared through the turnover target figures and my fellow shareholders, and I received the second payment.

This is how we used it...

I called the directors together and explained the situation. I asked them to take some time on their own and answer these two questions in writing.

I suggested they go forward in their mind to the point when we should have reached the turnover target figures, namely, March of the following year. And imagine we had <u>not</u> reached the target and would not get the second tranche of the earn-out money.

I wanted them to <u>feel the emotion</u> at that future point. And then, and only then, when they were in that emotional state, to write down their answers to this question:

"If only I'd... we would've reached the target.

What are those dots?"

You'll notice this is; "If only I'd...", <u>not</u> if only we, not if only the government, not if only the weather, not if only the financial situation, not if; anything other than personal responsibility.

Then, once they had written down as many ideas as they could think of, to change their mental state (perhaps take a walk, have a coffee, do or think something else), they sat down again, pad and pen in hand.

Bringing It All Together

Again, they would mentally go forward to the point when the target should have been reached, and this time, rather than imagine we missed it, they would imagine we had smashed it!

They would feel the elation, the joy, the power, the sheer exhilaration of having soared through the target and, of course, earning the second payment.

And when in that state, they would answer a fresh question:

"I reached the target because I...

What are those dots?".

And this time, knowing they helped us reach the target, they were <u>not</u> trying to re-create the opposite of the previous list of answers; but simply checking in their mind to see if they might have missed another powerful idea.

The combination of these two sets of answers gave us a complete list of actions each director had to individually take to ensure we successfully reached our goal.

When the directors returned and gave me their individual answer sheets, I added them to my own thoughts and spent the rest of the day creating a daily action plan (for every single working day) from that day in September all the way through to the 31st of March the following year.

Every morning from then on, before we started work, we checked the daily plan and stuck to the actions we'd agreed to take - and that's what enabled us to soar through the figures and receive the second tranche of the money.

paid!

Over the years since that success, I've used The Yesterday's Road Method in many different areas of my life: from reducing my golf handicap to reaching fitness and weight goals, from writing books to hitting sales targets.

And I've shared it with numerous clients who have reported back to me just how powerful the idea is and how helpful in being certain of the actions they need to take to achieve any goal.

I would urge you to use it. Here is a template to make it easier.

The Yesterday's Road Method:

The Yesterday's Road Method –Part 1

The date is...
and I have NOT achieved my goal of...
If only I'd...

paid!

The Yesterday's Road Method -Part 2

The date is...
and I have achieved my goal of...
Because I...

The Measure:

"You can't manage what you don't measure"

Now we need to measure our actions' results to discover whether they have taken us closer to our goal.

If they have, and we're still certain this is still the goal we want to achieve, then we will continue to take those actions.

If they are not taking us closer to the goal, and we're still certain this is the goal we want to achieve, then we need to consider different actions or a greater level of activity with the actions we've already decided upon.

There are other considerations.

It may be that now we have started to take action, we realise this is <u>not</u> a goal we want to achieve. So, therefore, we go back to the beginning of the process to establish exactly what it is we want.

If we still feel the goal is the right goal and the actions are the right actions, then we will need to examine the plan. Then we need to decide whether or not there are additional actions to be taken.

Are there other people who need to take action to help us? Or do we need more knowledge, experience, practice, or a variety of other factors you are aware of which may have come into play?

Perhaps, unforeseen obstacles have raised their heads, and they will take time, effort, and possibly money to solve them.

As you have seen from the WWHAM diagram, there is a clear feedback loop from action back to the goal (what), and by regularly reviewing the results of our activities, we ensure we are staying on track.

Internal and External

On the left hand side of the WWHAM diagram you can see the words - internal and external. It is important that we take time to use these in our measurements.

External refers to our external results, namely, the tangible results we have received. The amount of money, the numbers, the dates, the percentages, even the level of applause.

Internal refers to - how do we feel about those results? Are we excited and pleased about what we achieved so far? Are those feelings as expected? Better or worse?

I am certain that however large the tangible results; if I don't feel good about having achieved them; I am setting myself up for future problems and anxiety. Not something we want.

That's why I've included internal as well as external measurements and checking.

"Time and distance travelled compounds the effect of error"

Peter Thomson

The Measurement Mistake:

One of the mistakes I see in 'Measurement' is that measurement is made too soon in the process.

For example:

A marketing campaign takes place, and a certain number of orders are received. Unfortunately, the value of the orders does not meet the cost of the campaign, and it could be easy to think - the campaign is a failure.

However, as in most businesses, the majority of the turnover and profit is made from <u>repeat</u> business; we need to wait until backend sales have taken place to measure whether or not the initial campaign was profitable, or not.

I've seen, unfortunately, a great deal of initial spending wasted when this 'backend' marketing does not take place, in the mistaken belief the campaign did not work.

So there we have it, The WWHAM Process, a simple and highly effective way to set and measure our progress towards our goals.

paid!

WWHAM

Date   Who

What *do you want to achieve? (Be specific. Numbers, dates, etc)*

Why *do you want to achieve this? (Away and towards)*

How *are you going to achieve this?*

Action *List the actions you will take, including dates for completion.*

Measure *What measurement systems will you put in place?*

Bringing It All Together

The Three Business Activities:

In any business, three activities must be undertaken. These fit extremely well into the WWHAM Process. They are making, marketing, and measuring.

In any business, somebody is 'making ' the product or service of the business, and this area will have its own why, what, how, and measure.

Somebody is involved in the business's sales and marketing, and, again, this will have its own why, what, how, and measure.

Remember, throughout the business, measurement needs to be taken.

One of the exciting parts of measurement is calculating the different levels of turnover and profit that can be achieved by testing different fee rates, deluxe offerings, and additional products and services.

REFRESHER 10

1. Bringing It All Together.

2. Creating Focus.

3. Using WWHAM - why, what, how, action, measure.

4. If you don't know where you're going all the roads lead there.

5. A goal without a plan is just a wish.

6. The Yesterday's Road Method.

7. Asking, if only I'd...? Asking, because I...?

8. You can't manage what you don't measure.

9. Time and distance travelled compounds is the effect of error.

10. Measuring too soon can lead to false conclusions.

11. The three business activities. Making, marketing and measuring.

Action Plan

Actions	Priority	When by	Done

CHAPTER ELEVEN

What Might Stop You?

Raising your fee rates and implementing the ideas I've shared with you can seem like the start of a challenging journey.

However, as we take our first cautious steps on this new path, test and measure our results, we soon find our confidence increasing, like a well-exercised muscle, and we feel empowered to achieve even more.

Having faced the difficulty of starting from scratch and needing to make money to support my family, myself and my marketing efforts I truly understand how difficult it can be to step out of our comfort zones.

But with the courage of our convictions, knowing we deliver tremendous value, and realising there is a vast pool of potential clients just waiting for our help, we can be bold and enjoy the challenge.

paid!

In this chapter, I'm going to ask you to start by interacting with me on two levels at the same time.

1. As the reader of the ideas. Recognising those that resonate with you and your thoughts. Taking inspiration and courage from the methods. Knowing you can implement them and enjoy greater rewards..

2. Learning the formula I'm using to convey my ideas so you too can use this as a template to create the content you wish to share.

The 6 Stage Scripting System ...

This is the one I often use to create lead magnets. It's the one I employed for The 7 BIG Mistakes Report I mentioned earlier

Here's the formula:

1. Perspective
   So our reader can more readily associate and link our ideas with what they already know; it make sense to open the files in their minds. We do this by giving a perspective or context to the ideas we are about to share. I've already done this for you, in the preceding paragraphs.

2. Problem
   When we state the problem in clear, concise terms so the reader can identify with it.

3. Pain
    We explain the pain the problem creates. And where possible, we give examples of this to build the emotion attached to this pain. Why? Because this will inspire the reader to want to find out what solutions we can offer.

4. Possible Solutions
    Then we list the solutions that directly solve the problem we described in Point 2. We detail what needs to be done and offer suggestions to counteract any difficulties that may be met along the way.

5. Pleasure
    Now we explain the benefits and the "what's in it for them" so the reader has clarity about <u>why</u> taking the action would be a good idea. After all: "Resistance is created through a lack of clarity"

6. Plan of Action
    And finally, we give the reader a clear plan of action, so they can be confident they can deal with the problem and experience the upsides of their actions.

Now, using this formula, I'll explain the first of these challenges so you can apply and benefit from all of the ideas we've been through together in the PAID! book.

For the subsequent challenges, now you know the formula, I'll simply give you my suggestions for the actions you can take.

Problem #1: Lack of Confidence

1. Pain
   1. Embarrassment
   2. Missed opportunities
   3. Reduced income

2. Possible Solutions
   1. Build confidence by starting with small, manageable tasks that allow for early success.
   2. Focus on positive reinforcement and feedback to help build your self-belief.
   3. Reflect regularly on your achievements and progress.

3. Pleasure
   1. Increased feeling of self-worth.
   2. Looking forward to engaging with new clients and happy to spend time meeting others and explaining what you can do for them .
   3. Increased opportunities.
   4. Increased income leading to...
   5. Increased freedom of choice

4. Plan of Action
   1. Recognise the areas where you've felt a lack of confidence in the past.
   2. Recognise the areas where you feel you might experience a lack of confidence in the future.
   3. Recognise the problems and personal downsides that past lack of confidence has created for you.

4. Recognise the problems and personal downsides that future lack of confidence will create for you.
5. Decide you are going to be confident and commit to being so
6. Immediately do something that requires you to be confident.
    1. Call someone you've been putting off calling.
    2. Film a video explaining one of your ideas.
    3. Decide to write your book and write the order form for it.
    4. Whatever you know needs confidence for you to undertake the action

Problem #2: Resistance to Change

1. Make the transition easier by breaking down each of the new methods you're going to use; into manageable steps.
2. Recognise the numerous benefits you can enjoy, and relate these changes to your personal and business goals.
3. Re-read the examples I've shared with you of the successful implementation of these methods. These can offset any fears or concerns you have about taking action.

Problem #3: Overwhelm

1. Instead of trying to introduce many changes at once, introduce new ideas or methods one at a time.
2. Allow for adequate time to digest and practice each new concept before moving on to the next.
3. Keep clear records to recognise the positive impact on your results or noting what may need to be adjusted to improve results.

Problem #4: Lack of Time

1. Use the numerous time management techniques that are available (such as prioritising tasks or delegating responsibilities)
2. Calculate the long term time-saving potential of these ideas or methods, realising how initial time investment can lead to greater efficiencies later.
3. As you and I know; there is no such thing as time management. It can only be self-management by deciding what we will do with our irreplaceable time.
4. Recognise and then avoid any victim language you might inadvertently been using. (Such as: He keeps me on the phone for ages)

Problem #5: Fear of Failure

1. View failure as a learning opportunity rather than something to be feared.
2. If we consider the results of our actions as simply that; results from which we can learn; then we

encourage ourselves to be bold and take action knowing we can discover a new way to succeed.

3. Use the idea of "failing forward" and celebrate your effort and your learning, not just your successes.

Problem #6: Misalignment with Personal Values or Goals:

1. Spend time understanding your personal values and goals.
2. Align these new ideas or methods with these values.
3. This makes the methods feel more relevant and acceptable to you.
4. Check your feelings about the use of the methods as well as your tangible results. There's little point gaining extra results but feeling bad about them.

Problem #7: Insufficient Practice or Reinforcement:

1. Create opportunities to practice the new methods and receive feedback from friends or colleagues.
2. You'll recall the quote I mentioned earlier: "Amateurs practise till they get it right. Professionals practise till they cannot get wrong"
3. Recognise where your actions aren't producing the results you want.
4. Break down the practice into very short sections where you can improve one step at a time.
5. Then stitch all the sections together and practice the whole idea/method or script

Problem #8: Lack of Accountability:

1. Set up a system of accountability, such as regular progress self-meeting. Plug this into your calendar or diary system.
   "Record breakers are the people who keep records. The others are simply guessing"
2. Find an accountability partner among your colleagues or friends
3. Buddy-up with a member of the PAID! community

In the next chapter, I'll explain a number of extra ways of increasing your success so you can rightfully enjoy al the benefits of being rewarded for the positive impact your make to your clients lives.

If you have any questions about the implementation of the ideas and methods just email your question to:

success@peterthomson.com

REFRESHER 11

1. What Might Stop You?

2. Lack of confidence

3. Resistance to change

4. Overwhelm

5. Lack of time

6. Fear of failure

7. Misalignment with personal values or goals

8. Insufficient practice or reinforcement

9. Lack of accountability

CHAPTER TWELVE

Increasing Your Success

Now we have discussed so many different tried, tested, and proven ideas and methods, you can increase your rewards from the positive differences you make for your clients. So now is the time to consider how to further increase your success.

Private Practice

In my private practice (you remember this expression), I help a small number of consultants increase their recognition in their chosen marketplace and increase their incomes and the enjoyment level they get from their activities.

If you are interested in having a conversation about working together, simply drop me an email at: success@ peterthomson.com

paid!

If you have decided the time has come when you are going to write your business book and are considering what you need to do in the 4 key areas of creating, converting, cashing, and choosing - and feel you need some help...

Then put your answers in this survey and let me know what help you want. My team and I would be delighted to help you reach your goal.

Survey Link:
https://www.surveymonkey.com/r/thepaidbook

The Four Areas:

Creation:

This is where you take your knowledge, experience, expertise, and your take on all of those and create the manuscript for your book. It is just a matter of cascading the ideas from your mind into a digital source so they can subsequently be repurposed in a variety of ways.

Converting:

This is the area where all of the ideas you've captured are converted into a tips booklet, a book, and possibly even a report at this early stage. This will include such items as cover design, graphics, ISBN, layout, and printing.

Cashing:

This is when you reap the rewards of your hard work and generate a stream of qualified leads for your main activity, sell copies of your book, and begin to consider the different informational products you can create.

Choosing:

The whole purpose of being involved in the information exchange business via your main activity and informational products is to start the process (and enjoy) building a business and a life of choice.

This is when you have freedom <u>from</u> anything that may have held you back and freedom <u>to</u> be, do, and have whatever you set your heart and mind upon.

paid!

Here are a variety of recorded training programmes that may match what you're looking to achieve.

- How to run successful membership and subscription programmes
- How to run profitable promotional webinars
- Persuasion in print and in person

https://www.theacceleratorsclub.com/
subscription-and-membership-programs

https://www.theacceleratorsclub.com/
promotional-webinars

https://www.theacceleratorsclub.com/persuasion

Action Plan

Actions	Priority	When by	Done

paid!

A friend asked...

If I would write the introduction for his book.

I remember the day I sat to write it. I have no idea where the words came from; they just poured out onto the screen.

The Forgotten - The Remembered
Peter Thomson

There is a moment in every person's life
When the awareness of their destiny
Bursts, like a bubble, onto the surface of their conscious mind.

It is at that moment, the weak avoid the realisation,
And tasting the bitterness of regret,
Busy themselves with the mundane task of their lives.

It is also at that moment, the strong awake!
And sensing the tingle of commitment made,
Decide to take the actions to change the world, their world, for the better...

And by so doing, secure for themselves
Their rightful and valued place in the history of humankind

Now, is that moment!

The Next Step:

You now have my complete guide on how you can continue to make a positive difference for your clients (and in the world) and, as a result, get rightfully, regularly and substantially rewarded for your impact.

I wish you ongoing success in all your adventures in life and look forward to the day when we meet to share our experiences.

Peter

Peter Thomson
"The UK's Most Prolific Information Product Creator"

Peter Thomson Bio

Peter Thomson is regarded as The UK's Leading Strategist on Business and Personal Growth and The UK's Most Prolific Information Product Creator.

Starting in business in 1972 he built 3 successful companies – selling the last to a public company, after only 5 years trading, for £4.2M enabling him to retire at age 42.

Since that time Peter has concentrated on sharing his proven methods for business and personal success via online video programmes, books, seminars, conference speeches and mentoring programmes.

With over 100 audio and 100 video programmes written and recorded he is Nightingale Conant's leading UK author.

paid!

In 1999 The American Intercontinental University in London – with permission granted by the American Government- awarded Peter an Honorary Doctorate (Doctor of Letters) for his work in communication skills and helping others to succeed in life. And in 2017 Peter was also awarded a lifetime achievement award by the ISM (Institute of Sales Management)

Peter specialises in helping coaches, consultants, speakers, trainers and small-business owners share more of their authentic messages with more people than they could ever reach on a 1-to-1 basis by showing them how to write and create and market their own informational products and charge the right fee rates.

To talk to Peter, send an email his Marketing Manager Rachel Groves:
rachel@peterthomson.com or call +44 (0) 7910 582539

Here's a link to Peter's YouTube channel, so you can see Peter's engaging style:
https://www.youtube.com/@PeterThomson/videos

Testimonials

And here are just a few testimonials from previous clients Peter has worked with:

I was a member of Peter's membership programme and also had monthly 1 to 1 sessions at Peter's home (highly recommended!)

Soon into the programme Peter helped me to focus on producing an online video-based product as my strength is presenting and training.

To cut a long story short, through Peter's invaluable, informal and fun mentoring I now have a video programme, the Limbic Performance System (LPS), which has changed my life. I no longer need to train unless I want to, and LPS made around £250,000 in just 1 year from its launch.

Estimated blended sales in the 12 months following were over £1,000,000 **- Steve Neale - BCS International Ltd**

"Working with Peter over a period of 18 months I created additional profits of over £100,000 using his ideas." **- Mark Wickersham, Accountant**

This book is impossible to read – I've tried several times and failed. Even getting to the end of a chapter is a struggle.

It's packed with such a wealth of practical approaches, brilliant ideas, and real-life solutions you have just have to put it down and take immediate action.

paid!

Written in Peter's distinctive style, not business book language, its instantly accessible and relatable for any consultant or advisor wishing to move their business forward.

So read it through once quickly, then read it a second time slowly with a notebook book to hand for your actions, but I doubt if you'll resist working on them for long.

The advice and guidance here is of immeasurable value and an incredible source of inspiration. **Stephen Dann - Business Impact Solutions**

Pay very close attention to what Peter has to say.

One of his insights alone has had a profound effect on my business:

Turnover before I met Peter: £79,672
Then one year later £267,172
And in the second year £384,442
and that's from just implementing ONE of Peter's suggestions.

If you feel that you are not being rewarded sufficiently for your efforts then you must read PAID! " **Sylvia Snowling - SDLT Claims Ltd**

TEMPLATES:

To make this as easy as possible for you to take action with the ideas and methods you'll discover throughout paid!, I've created a number of templates. These are the templates I use in my private practice and those I share with my clients.

Go to: www.thepaidbook.com/downloads where you can access them.

If you have any questions about the use of the templates – email success@peterthomson.com

Accreditation:

With thanks to...

Dan Sullivan - Strategic Coach
www.strategiccoach.com

Joe Polish – Genius Network
www.geniusnetwork.com

Prof. Robert Cialdini – Influence at Work
www.influenceatwork.com

Roy H Williams – The Wizard of Ads
www.rhy.com

Get Your FREE Copy

Because you're a reader of **paid!**
You're entitled to your FREE copy of the essential

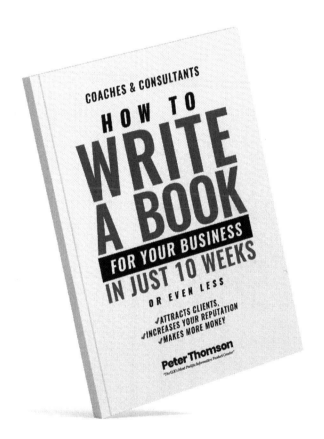

Simply go to:
www.thepaidbook.com/downloads

Printed in Great Britain
by Amazon

35028091R00145